THE TECHNIQUE OF
Handling People

BOOKS BY DONALD A. LAIRD AND ELEANOR C. LAIRD

Practical Sales Psychology
Practical Business Psychology
Sizing Up People
The Technique of Getting Things Done
The Technique of Personal Analysis
The Technique of Building Personal Leadership
The Technique of Handling People, Revised Edition
The Psychology of Selecting Employees

PUBLISHED BY HARPER & BROTHERS
Increasing Personal Efficiency

PUBLISHED BY FUNK & WAGNALLS COMPANY
The Strategy of Handling Children

PUBLISHED BY AMERICAN BANKERS ASSOCIATION
Human Relations in Banking

THE TECHNIQUE OF

Handling People

ELEVEN HELPS
for Your Human Relations

Donald A. Laird, PH.D., SC.D.
AND Eleanor C. Laird

McGRAW-HILL BOOK COMPANY, INC.
New York   Toronto   London

THE TECHNIQUE OF HANDLING PEOPLE

REVISED EDITION

TWELFTH PRINTING

36029

Library of Congress Catalog Card Number: 54-6225

Published by the McGraw-Hill Book Company, Inc.

Printed in the United States of America

PREFACE

Human Relations has made big strides as a science. But the average man or woman has not made equal gains in personal human relations. There is a big gap between how people actually get along with others, and how they might get along if they used modern principles of human relations.

This little book aims to help this average person to better relationships with others. The book originated from talks to supervisors and executives, sales people and teachers, clubwomen and luncheon clubs. The talks illustrated in a direct way some of the little things which modern research shows are big for human relations.

The first edition had what the publisher calls "an amazing record." Thirteen large printings. The book has been used in the armed forces, and for training salesmen and executives. Many copies have been used by the Holmes Institute in their leadership training programs, and also by them in cooperation with the Nippon Management Association of Japan. A German translation has been brought out by Albert Muller Verlag, Zurich.

In this second edition numerous small changes and additions have been made. In addition, a new first chapter has been added to give a perspective on what some consider the number one problem which today faces people in all walks of life.

Donald A. Laird
Eleanor C. Laird

"Homewood"

CONTENTS

(The key phrases are emphasized)

ELEVEN RULES FOR LEADERSHIP

ASK QUESTIONS

BE BRIEF

CONFIDENT BEARING

DIRECTNESS

EARNESTNESS

FRIENDLINESS

GOOD-FINDING

HARNESS CRITICISM

INCREASE OTHERS' SELF-ESTEEM

JINGLE PRAISE

KNOW YOUR PEOPLE

*These key rules can be easily
remembered, since they are arranged
alphabetically from A to K*

1 *Helps for your human relations*

It's a story worth recalling again. Benjamin was a nineteen-year-old with a good brain and a lot of confidence in himself. Generous too—when looking for a job he gave half of his worldly money to a beggar on the street. But he was headstrong, self-centered, uncooperative.

He ran away from his family in Boston because he had difficulty getting along with an older brother. Ben felt the brother was bossing him too much. Poor human relations with his family.

So here he was in Philadelphia, practically penniless. The chunky youth had plenty of ability, and enough ambition, and worked diligently.

But the going was rough for him. His criticism of others, arrogance, and arguing punctured any dreams he may have had about getting along with people.

It began to dawn on young Franklin that perhaps he was making mistakes in his handling of others. He took time to analyze his actions, to see what he might have been doing that lost him the good will and cooperation of others. And to figure better approaches for his human contacts.

No more obeying his first impulses (which are often childish impulses), but a *cultivated growth* as he gradually improved his methods for managing human relationships.

This cultivated growth made Franklin the most popular, and among the most influential residents of Philadelphia by the time he was thirty. At forty, he was able to retire from business and live in luxury on his income for forty-four more years.

Late in life he wrote about the guides he followed for his cultivated personal growth in relationships with people. You will find them in his *Autobiography*. Reading this has helped many profit by Franklin's experiences.

Human relations is a new phrase, but it describes something as old as the Garden of Eden. It refers to the state of affairs which exists between you and other people. You have human relationships whether you have been aware of them or not.

In everyday words, it means how well we get along with others. Our human relationships are in good condition when others cooperate willingly with us. When they like and appreciate us. When they give us their best efforts.

When they follow us without needing threats or bribes to "get them in line." When we get teamwork on the job, in our home, from fellow club members, and from neighbors.

Money doesn't count for much in human relations. Hetty Green was the richest woman at the turn of the century—and the most friendless, but for her dog. Clara Barton, an underpaid government clerk who lived at the same time, could influence people so effectively that she was able to found the American Red Cross. More about Miss Barton shortly.

Personal beauty and fashionable clothes do not have much to do with one's human relations. John Hancock was the best-dressed man of distinction about Boston— but sloppily dressed Paul Revere had vastly better human relations. The big businesses which Hancock inherited failed under his management. But some of the businesses which Revere started are still going today, as we will learn in a moment.

What does count in human relationships, as shown by a flood of reports from surveys and experiments, is the *human atmosphere*, or *human climate*. It is not tricks, or "sizzles," which hypnotize others. It is the way we change the human atmosphere so that people feel friendly rather than hostile, so they come to us rather than avoid us.

If there is one secret in handling people it is to generate an atmosphere in which others feel at ease, and appreciated, and among friends. In the following chapters we will describe eleven techniques which help improve the human atmosphere.

For the present, we will mention only two general factors in this climate.

1. The attitudes you show toward others, and which you may show without realizing it.
2. The methods you use when you handle people.

"Natural impulses" are not always good guides. It is

"natural" for one man to belittle others, and just as "natural" for another man to give others encouragement.

Unfortunately, people are not born with instincts which guide them to do the best things for good human relations—as the history of the world, and of some companies, indicates.

The classic survey of office employees, by veteran business educator H. Chandler Hunt, showed that only 24 per cent of the employees were held back from promotion because they did not know the details of the higher job. Most of them were not promoted because they had glaring weaknesses in their human relationships in the office.

Fortunately, a swarm of scientific studies in the field of human relations does point the way with guides for a better handling of people. These guides are easier for some people to catch on to and use than for others.

Let's see what business leaders think about this.

General Motors Corp. keeps reminding its executives that it takes followers to make a leader.

Modern business emphasizes human relations because the supervisor, or manager, gets work done through people. Teamwork is essential all up and down the line.

But human relations are likely to be strained when people have to be asked to do things which they had not planned themselves, or which they may not be keen to do. Bosses—and parents—have to do many things which go "against the grain" in handling workers or children.

But there is less strain on human relations when such unavoidable duties are done in a favorable human atmosphere. An example is two small factories that were surveyed by Dr. May Smith, an industrial psychologist. The two plants made the same articles, and had the same wage scales. But their general managers set very different human atmospheres.

The manager of one plant was a slave driver and watchdog—authoritarian. Apparently he never dreamed of such a thing as human relations. His workers had a quit rate of 55 per cent a year.

The competing plant, practically identical except that its manager set a more democratic atmosphere, had a quit rate of only 15 per cent a year.

Many similar surveys have shown that the supervisor who establishes a favorable human atmosphere has fewer absences from work, fewer accidents, and often better production. Findings such as those have prompted business leaders to say the following things about good human relations' attitudes and methods.

"The most important single ingredient in the formula of success is knowing how to get along with people," was the way Theodore Roosevelt valued it. He had to work at it, for "by nature" he inclined to be too bossy for his own good.

Stanley C. Allyn, who started work peddling papers, worked his way through school, and became president of the National Cash Register Co., said: "Today the most useful person in the world is the man or woman who knows how to get along with other people. Human relations is the most important science in the broad curriculum of living."

Edwin J. Thomas went to work with Goodyear Tire & Rubber Co. as an extra clerk when he was seventeen. At forty-one he became president of the largest rubber company in the world. "Friendly, kindly guidance wins cooperation which is more to be desired than subservience or meekness," was his human relations philosophy.

A small-town Ohio boy who worked up to the presidency of the International Harvester Co., John L. McCaffrey, put it this way: "Every businessman needs to learn how to get along with other human beings, both as individuals and as groups. Some of that knowledge can come only through experience, but much of it can be taught."

C. Donald Dallas left high school after one year—but returned after working three years because he wanted to finish the scientific course. Then he learned the brass business from the bottom up. He reorganized, and later became president of, the brass and copper business that was started by Paul Revere. Dallas' human relations practice was to "establish, through every possible means, the self-respect of workers and make them feel they're part of the team—not just numbers on a time clock."

President McCaffrey said that much of human relations can be taught. Our everyday activities can be a laboratory where we test the teachings.

An increasing number of corporations are setting up departments for training in democratic human relations. This has been taught at the West Point Military Academy since 1946, in a course on military psychology. This course was started upon the request of the then chief of staff, Dwight Eisenhower.

The New York Central System has used a special correspondence course to train more than 7,000 supervisors in better human relations practices and atmosphere.

The Southern Pacific Lines has an assistant to the president to arrange classes for employees along their 15,188 miles of railroad. President Armand T. Mercier, who started with the lines as a surveyor, said, "Business finds it relatively easy to obtain technically skilled workers; but the great need is for men who can organize, inspire, and harmonize the work of others."

The American Bankers Association has had a special course prepared to guide conferences in the field of human relations which are held by some of the 300,000 bank staff members across the country.

Police departments, and retailers, are giving quickie courses on human relations and handling people. The strong national sales organizations bear down heavily on this.

Large-scale training in the better handling of people is under way in earnest.

But what can the person do who does not work for an organization that gives courses in human relations—yet?

For one thing, he can do just as you are doing now—he can read about the applications of other people's experiences, and the findings of modern research in group dynamics and interpersonal relations.

Shortly after Franklin retired at forty, a freckle-faced teen-ager in Virginia contemplated his own future. It did not seem optimistic. He carefully worked out for himself some *Rules of Conduct* to guide him in getting along with others.

This shy, bashful Virginia boy would have to carve his own future, and he made a sensible start by schooling himself in human relations—cultivated growth, again. Perhaps you have seen those fifty-seven rules which George Washington wrote out for his own guidance, and which he carried with him for years. You can read them, with his original misspellings, at page 17 of our book *The Technique of Personal Analysis.*

As Harvey Firestone commented, "When you find yourself working hard and accomplishing little, stop and analyze yourself." There are good chances you will find that little blunders have given rise to a human atmosphere that has unduly complicated life for you.

Here's another way for getting a new start in human relations—marry the right person. That was what Andrew Carnegie did, although he married more with love in mind.

The peppy little Scot was a smart trader who could smell a chance to make money miles away. He had tried to get loyalty by paying fabulous salaries to his managers. Bribing rather than winning cooperation.

After their wedding his socialite wife took him in hand to correct some of his blunders in getting along with people. There was his habit of talking so much that others could not get a word in edgewise.

"Give others more chance to talk," she told him. "When I pretend to smooth the front of my blouse, that will be a signal for you to stop and let the other person talk. Just ask him a question to get him started, then listen without interrupting." (More about asking questions in the next chapter.)

Another of her signals was a swish of her skirt when he was bragging about himself. That swish was a sign he should switch his talk and give the other person some credit. (More about others' self-esteem in Chapter 10.)

Those signals worked wonders for Carnegie. Before his marriage people held him in awe and fear. People had been interested in him for the money they might get out of him. But after the blouse-smoothing and skirt-swishing and other signals had changed the way he handled people, he became one of the most popular and admired men of his day.

Perhaps rich people, and those with big salaries, have more need for good human relations than the rest of us do. Envy, you know.

There are several other conditions in which the need for human relations is increased. Factory and office workers, for instance, have more need than farmers or hermits.

If you have to give orders, or help people reach decisions, the need goes up. Here are examples of some

walks of life in which extra helps in human relations are
usually needed:

Attorneys	Physicians
Clergymen	Policemen
Club officers, or aspiring	Politicians
officers	Salespeople of all kinds
Dentists	Service people
Military officers	Social workers
Morticians	Supervisors and managers
	Teachers

There are in addition a few varieties of people who
need to give special attention to their human relations,
regardless of their occupations. For instance, the small percentage who are so aggressive, or bossy, that they rub
the fur the wrong way. Franklin, at nineteen, was an example of how this sets the wrong human atmosphere.

Some ambitious people also. They may be so eager to
get ahead that they neglect to cultivate the very methods
of handling others that would help them up the ladder.

As evidence, Dr. Daniel Starch analyzed 50 lower executives and compared them with 50 top executives. The
average top executive earned twenty times as much as
the average lower executive. The top executive rated 87
per cent on ability to handle people, while the lower ones
rated only 23 per cent. Good handling of people smooths
the way for the ambitious—helps them realize their po-
tentials.

Impulsive, quick-acting people also tend to strain their
human relations. They act, then may regret. That was

Carnegie's weakness. They particularly need some guides to make their hasty actions more favorable.

And don't overlook the pitfalls for the person who has a marked streak of hostility—envy, jealousy, rivalry, mistrust. In our competitive world it seems as if these characteristics become overdeveloped readily. But they make one slide down the human relations ladder—as in John Hancock's case.

There are several times in your life cycle, or business career, when your human relations will be under more stress than usual. Here are some of these crisis times:

When reporting on a new job.

When a new worker is placed beside you, or joins your department, or you get a new boss.

When you are promoted, but your fellow workers are not. Or vice versa.

When you move into a new neighborhood, or join a new club.

The first few months after you are married.

From the time your children enter the sixth grade until they finish high school.

The first few months after one of your children is married.

When you are tired or excited (overhasty).

When something seems to be blocking your ambitions.

When you are criticized.

When you are with, or talking about, people you dislike (hostility).

When you become old and set in your ways. This

happened when Clara Barton reached eighty—the American Red Cross nearly fell apart under her authoritarian management in her older years.

Watch your attitudes and methods (techniques) in those critical periods.

From time to time you will bump into a person who is in some way especially difficult to get along with. Such as imperious John Hancock, or Franklin when he was in his "argumentative period." Or you may have to put up with an old-style boss who confuses bulldozing with managing.

It has been estimated that perhaps one person out of every ten is "just naturally" ornery and difficult to get along with. Since you can't evade these ornery folk forever, might as well make the best use of human relations rules when they block your path.

As George Washington wrote to General Philip Schuyler, "We must make the best of mankind as they are, since we cannot have them as we wish."

Now for a bit of bad news—which should be a challenge. There seems to be more need for help in human relationships today. Social scientists believe two changes in our world have made these relations acute.

1. Population congestion has increased so that most of us are hemmed in by other people.
2. Self-employment has declined so that 80 per cent of us now have to work as team members, with and for other people.

Those are some of the reasons why publicist Edward L. Bernays said "Human relations is the number-one problem of the twentieth century."

Henry Ford was a mechanical genius, but set an authoritarian atmosphere which bungled many of his human contacts. Grandson Henry Ford II, who carried the family firm to greater heights, observed: "If we can solve the problem of human relationships in industrial production, I believe we can make as much progress toward lower costs during the next ten years as we made during the past quarter century through the development of mass production."

Each year now the Ford Foundation is appropriating enormous sums for research and projects in human relations, not only in industrial work but also in family, community, and international spheres.

Here is how it looks to the chairman of General Mills, Inc., Harry A. Bullis, who started as a bookkeeper. "During the early years of this century, expansion and production occupied the best business brains. The years between the two world wars were characterized by tremendous emphasis on selling and merchandising. The second half of our century will be marked by inspiring progress in the field of human relations."

Frank W. Abrams, a civil engineer who had to pick up human relations for himself, worked his way up to the chairmanship of the Standard Oil Company of New Jersey. This is what he told graduating engineers: "During the past thirty-five years the time that managements have been devoting to human relations problems has been vastly increased, until today the manager is apt to spend more hours on such problems than on any others."

Chairman Abrams went on, "Perhaps the time that our engineering schools give to studying the stresses and strains of humans should be greatly increased."

We have seen that many great leaders saw this challenge, and met it by figuring out their own guide rules. Some of these guides have stood the test of time—the wisdom we might glean from the ages.

But there is always a danger that the rule one figures out for oneself may be merely a justification for some impulsive practices one can't avoid. Bossy people, for example, have sometimes concluded that the best way to handle people is to "keep them guessing." We now know that is a dangerous leadership practice.

Fortunately there are now many scientifically established guides which can be followed with confidence. The first official research center for the study of human relations was established in the U.S., in 1944, at the Massachusetts Institute of Technology. There had been much work before this, but this was the first large-scale center. Now there are a couple dozen in this country, and a few abroad. Millions of dollars are being invested in their researches, including government funds. Our style of military leadership has been profoundly affected by some of the findings.

Where can the average person learn about these findings?

Since 1948 there has been an international journal *Human Relations*, which is published jointly by The Research Center for Group Dynamics at the University of Michigan, and The Travistock Institute of Human Relations, London, England. Other technical journals on psychology, sociology, and education carry the overflow.

All this work in interpersonal relations has revolutionized many old ideas. But with scientific advances, special vocabularies have been devised which you will not find in the dictionaries. A report which is rich in value to the average person may be about as meaningless to him as if it had been written in antique Latin.

Some companies have broken this bottleneck by having consultants translate the findings into everyday language, pointing up possible applications for that particular firm. These reports are circulated up and down the executive ladder, and occasionally company-wide conferences are held on them.

A special effort to train group leaders for this work is made at a summer course by the National Training Laboratory in Group Development. This course is usually restricted to people fairly well up the ladder. The course is given in Maine, but the headquarters are at 1201 Sixteenth St., N.W., Washington 6, D.C.

The Social Science Reporter, a little magazine issued twice a month, gives a digest of research for top management. The subscription price of this four-page report is $250 a year. It is published at 365 Guinda St., Palo Alto, Calif.

But how about the majority of us who do not have a spare $250, and are bumping elbows on human relations problems daily? Well, you don't read the medical journals, do you? But you do learn much about good health practices from news items and health columns in the newspapers. Or from magazine articles and books for the non-medical person.

Just so with findings in research in the field of human relations. Most daily papers have a column on psychology from which you can get helps. Columns for parents also give useful human relations advice from time to time.

Many of the social-science textbooks used in high school—even junior high—give easy-to-understand summaries of progress in human relations principles. Read some of those chapters—after the children have gone to bed, if you don't want them to catch you.

Trade and business magazines are giving more and more space to accounts of this work. Many trade journals have one article on this topic in each issue, even journals devoted to chemical engineering.

There are not many books in this field for the general reader which jibe with scientific findings. Much plausible nonsense and many "inspirational messages" are definitely off the beam. Probably your safest guide in choosing a popular book in this field is to ask, not your neighbor, but the department of psychology at the nearest large university. The next safest is to make certain the book was written by a member of the American Psychological Association or the American Sociological Society. The book may not be as peppy and make as many promises as the other one, but it will doubtless carry you further in the long run.

And, for good measure, throw in some of the wisdom of the ages from Franklin's *Autobiography* and Washington's *Rules of Conduct.*

From here on we will show how to use eleven practical techniques which will improve the human atmosphere for your relations with others—provided you gradually make each technique a habit. There will be a separate chapter for each technique, so you may want to read one chapter, then practice the technique it explains, before going on to the next.

We will talk about "you" often—to secure your ego-involvement, as the technical reports would say it.

Several actual examples will be used to show how each technique is worked. A variety of examples is used, so that some of them will be right down your street—fit your frame of reference, in the technical reports.

You will likely catch the idea quickly in each chapter. We have simplified the practices to their lowest common denominator to make them as clear as possible.

So that you will more likely remember, and also act on the principles, we have used examples with human interest in them. A heartthrob is also tucked in here and there for the same purposes. So, from now on this may seem more like a storybook than an ordinary textbook. We hope so, for then it should produce greater changes in you. After all, the human atmosphere you create depends more upon your attitudes and feelings than on odds and ends of facts you can repeat glibly.

Have you ever wondered why some leaders ask so many questions? The first general practice we will take up is how to ask what kind of questions.

2 ASK QUESTIONS
to win cooperation

If you are expecting something complicated, change your mind.

The secrets of handling people are simple and obvious when we get down to essentials. Consider, for instance, how the Butler firm got its toughest competition.

A young boy went to work for the firm, direct from high school. He was put in the shipping room, where he could learn something about the company's finished products. His job was packing unfinished castings into heavy wooden boxes.

The castings had rough edges and had to be handled with leather gloves. Since the raw edges would soon wear through gloves and into knuckles, sticks were used to tamp down the straw that was placed around the castings to prevent joggling. Young White wore out a couple of tamping sticks a day and had to cut new ones out of scrap lumber.

One afternoon he was leaning against a shipping case, whittling a smooth handle on a new tamping stick. The new plant superintendent came in on his first visit to the shipping department.

The new superintendent was an efficiency expert and was making the shop hum. He was so new in the plant, however, that he still had lots to learn about it—the use of tamping sticks, for instance, or how to lead people.

When he saw young White sitting and whittling, the superintendent glared at the lad. His eyes narrowed to angry slits, and he nodded his head threateningly.

The boy jumped to his feet, to tell about his tamping stick. But the superintendent spoke first.

"So you think you can get by with loafing and whittling on the job, just because nobody ever comes into the shipping room," he said coldly. "You're fired—right now. Get out!"

Twenty years later White told me of this experience. His face flushed and he fairly boiled as he repeated the superintendent's "Get out!"

White is now running Butler's strongest competitor. He makes it as tough as possible for that company, for he is still hopping mad at the one-time efficiency man.

"If I have any secret of managing men," White told me, "I learned it that afternoon, in Butler's shipping room. That unjust treatment burned into my soul the importance of asking questions, of getting information instead of jumping to conclusions, especially unfavorable conclusions, about my men.

"I ask so many questions," and he smiled at this, "that a couple of years ago, when our foremen's club put on a gridiron dinner, they had a man take me off. They called him the Human Question Mark; all he did was ask questions. It was a good take-off of me, all right.

"I didn't mind it at all, since it was done in a friendly spirit. And the men know that my questions prevent a lot of needless trouble. If that new superintendent at Butler's had asked me why I was whittling he would have learned something about the business, and chances are I might still be working *with* him right now.

"It helps in lots of ways, this asking questions. When I have a man who doesn't seem to be too certain of himself, who needs to have his confidence raised a bit, I *ask for his opinion* on something. It's amazing how that seems to set him up.

"Then, too, it works with fellows who are not co-operative, perhaps a bit on the ornery side. I *ask them to do me a little favor.* Last week, for instance, I asked a fellow who was getting out of line if he'd witness my signature on my driver's license application. It was a simple little thing, but he's a changed man in his attitude toward me now. I study quite a bit to figure up little favors to ask of someone who seems to be getting his back up at me."

"It worked in selling, too, this asking questions. I was on the road a couple of years, to learn all angles of the business. I dreaded doing this, for I'm not cut out for sales work. And I was making a good failure of it, until I took some time out to analyze what was wrong with me.

"I got hold of something by John Paterson—you know, he built up the National Cash Register Co. from practically nothing. He told his men not to try to sell on the first call—or on the second, either—until they had asked enough questions to know how their products could be best used by the firm.

"So I started asking our customers questions, instead of telling them how rapidly we were growing. You know, when I stopped doing most of the talking and just used suitable, sensible questions, the customer began to talk and the orders came to me.

"Several customers told me, in fact, that they liked the way I sold them, didn't use high pressure, and seemed to know what they needed. If I hadn't asked the questions, I'd have never known when they were ripe to buy. I landed some of our best customers that way—got them away from Butler—and they are still with us after ten years."

"But it is in handling complaints and gripes that asking questions pays the biggest rewards. You know, there is always a lot more to the complaint than the complainer usually talks about. You've got to get at the bottom of things, and nothing beats asking sensible, friendly questions to get at the facts.

"We had a meeting last week, for instance, over a job classification that was supposed to be too low. After some questions I found the men thought it should be rated higher because their supervisor, a conscientious young engineer, was watching them so closely that they had mistakenly concluded their job required more skill and training than was the case.

"When someone comes in all riled up, I find the best

way to get him cooled off is to ask questions. I first found this out when my oldest girl was just a kid. She'd come running home, crying mad, to tell what someone had done to her. I'd ask where they had been playing, who was there, and how she liked the game, and she'd forget her angry tears and excitedly tell me about her play. You'd scarcely think a person could change so quickly.

"I've had foremen come in so mad they could scarcely see, wanting an O.K. to fire someone. By asking questions and gradually steering them away from their gripe, most of them go back to the department and seem to forget the gripe, and that's one reason why we have low turnover of help. Then, you know, thinking ahead about the next question to ask keeps me so busy that I don't have a chance to catch their anger myself. It's a good way to keep cool."

Self-made White, who is an unusually capable leader of men, might have added that asking questions helps get better results in business deals, too. Thomas A. Edison learned this accidentally, early in his career. Businessmen who were interested in buying one of his first inventions called on him. He had expected to get, possibly, a few thousand for his invention. They asked him what he wanted for it.

Edison was about to mention the figure he had in mind, when, for some reason he did not understand, he asked, "Well, how much will you pay?"

The top-hatted men glanced at each other, and the

spokesman mentioned a price many times what Edison had in mind.

Thenceforth Edison never told prospects how much he wanted but asked what they would give.

Bear that in mind when your prospective employer wants to know the salary you expect.

As an aid in starting a conversation, try using questions, not questions such as "Are you comfortable?" which are answered by a single word, after which the topic is closed. Ask questions that will get the other fellow started on a story, such as:

"What was your first job?"

"How did you manage during the fuel shortage?"

"What was the most frightening experience you ever had?"

Talk never dies down when someone knows how to ask questions that get others relating some experience.

The right questions are first aid for the tongue-tied. Just ask questions so that others do most of the talking, and they will be telling their friends what a wonderful conversationalist you are—because you had them do most of the talking.

I was at a meeting recently at which an aerial gunner was the guest of honor. He had been in the thick of it in Pearl Harbor and at the battles of Midway and the Solomons. He had drifted for days on the ocean, after Jap Zeros had shot down his plane.

He had been decorated for bravery. But he lost his

bravery when he had a chance to talk to an eager group of sympathetic listeners. He would rather face a squadron of Jap fighter planes than the innocent little microphone of the public-address system.

For a few seconds, which seemed like quarter hours, the returned hero tried to think of something to say. He would have given anything to be back floating, hungry and scorched, on a life raft, away from that crowd. A bad case of stage fright.

"That's fine!" the chairman said as he came to the hero's rescue beside the microphone. "What friendly things did the natives do for you after they rescued you from the raft?"

When you have to give a talk, you may not have a friendly chairman to come to your rescue. But you will not need one if you ask yourself questions, in front of everybody, and then answer them.

Try it when outlining a speech. You'll probably give a better talk if you jot down some questions, then answer them one by one, as you would in conversation.

This is a positive book. We are interested in what people should do to be better leaders of others—and of themselves. The wrong things we shall mention seldom. It's better to keep our minds on the best ways. From time to time, however, it is wise to give passing mention to possible pitfalls. In asking questions, for instance:

Don't pry into personal affairs.

Don't ask questions unless you are pretty certain the person addressed can answer them.

Don't ask questions that seem to cross-examine.

Don't ask in an antagonizing way—make it friendly conversation.

Don't ask questions to show off yourself—ask those that help the other fellow show off.

You should know about *reverse questions*. They are the ones to use when questions are directed to you. An inexperienced salesman, for example, was making the common error of answering customers' questions completely—so that the sales interviews died on first base.

"Which pattern do you think I should get?" the customer would ask.

Now a smart leader would reverse that question and not try to answer it himself. He would reverse it—turn it back to the asker—by saying:

"Well, let me see, what will you be using it for?"

Edison learned early, as we have seen, to reverse questions. When asked how much he wanted for an invention he replied, "What will you offer me?"

In football terms, let the other fellow carry the ball while you direct the plays by reversing questions for him to answer.

Benjamin Franklin was an inveterate question asker and adept in reversing questions. So was Socrates. So are most leaders. Bosses tell them—leaders ask them.

Many people inwardly resent being told what to do. They usually carry out the orders, but halfheartedly.

They get their work done, but not in a spirit of co-operation. This is frequently because of the way they have been told what to do or how to do it.

Oscar, who was chuck-full of good ideas for his company, did not realize this fact as he presented one idea after another to his boss. The boss listened, looked wise, thanked him coolly—and none of Oscar's suggestions were put into effect.

Then Oscar learned about using questions. He changed his way of presenting ideas. "What would you think," he would ask the boss, "of making a window display of game sets along with tables on which to use the games?"

The boss took to the suggestions when they were given in that form, although he had turned many of them down when Oscar had said directly, "We ought to display these two together."

Bosses, after all, are just as human as the rest of us, and we have to use leadership with them as well as with those working for us.

And in handling those who work for us, a question is often better than a direct order or suggestion. People who have worked for Owen D. Young, of General Electric Company, for instance, claim he never gave orders. He would ask, "Could you do this?" or "Could we get out a report on this by the end of the week?"

This made people feel they were working with him, not for him. It got cooperation and not resentment. They weren't being bossed too obviously.

Young bosses, especially, are likely to err in being too

direct in their orders. Ask your subordinates, rather than tell them, and you will get better results in four instances out of five.

A trouble shooter in labor relations has an amazing record of getting at the bottom of things. He discovers reasons for trouble that had never been suspected. One simple question produces these almost miraculous results. After he has heard a person's story through he nods his head in understanding agreement, then he says, "and, in addition to that—?"

There is usually a pause until the complainer resumes. Until this "magic question" is asked, the complaints usually deal with vague things. But asking "and, in addition to that?" brings out things the complainer was almost ashamed to mention but which really were at the bottom of the trouble.

When you have trouble to deal with, or a disgruntled or complaining person to handle, end by asking that magic question.

It helps in sales, too. A young life insurance salesman had a large policyholder who wanted to lapse the policy. The policyholder said his status had changed so that he no longer needed the insurance, and that vague answer seemed to be the end of it. But Dick recalled the magic question, and asked, "and, in addition to that?" The man who wanted to lapse his policy hesitated, but Dick kept quiet.

Then the man told about his domestic troubles—his wife was getting a divorce. This meant he would no

THE BOSS WHO ASKED QUESTIONS
GOT BETTER RESULTS

**Per cent of workers
reporting it above average**

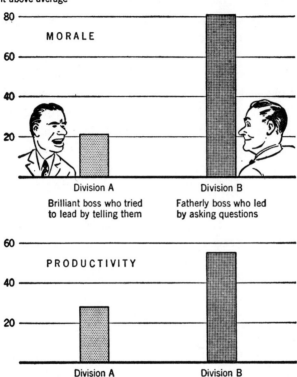

Government employees doing identical work, but under
bosses who used very different methods of leading, reported
on the morale and the estimated productivity of their divi-
sions. Data gathered for the Office of Naval Research by
Dr. Irving R. Weschler and associates in Institute of Industrial Relations of University of California, Los Angeles.

29

longer want the policy to provide for her. Knowing the real reason for the lapse, Dick was able to show how the policy could be converted into an endowment policy to provide for comforts in the man's middle years. He would probably never have learned this, until too late, without asking that magic question.

The same labor trouble shooter has another question of magical value. When the interview seems finished, he tilts back in his chair, as if settling down for a long, comfortable period, and asks, "What do you like best about your boss?" Sometimes he asks what the man likes best about the firm or his particular job.

This ends the interview in a constructive fashion. The man who was complaining an hour before is now briefly telling himself, as well as the labor relations man, that there are good points after all. It lets him leave the interview in a constructive, cooperative frame of mind. This question lets the men sell themselves.

Many salespeople have learned that the man they can't sell can sell himself. A young soap salesman came up against the sourest man in his new territory. The salesman did not know that for years this grocer had a hatred for his firm that bordered on the abnormal. So young William Wrigley, Jr., innocently walked into the store to sell this obstreperous proprietor a big order of soap.

"You and your company can go jump in the river," was the grocer's cheerful statement.

Wrigley started to shut his kit.

"Well, you know a lot about soap and how to sell it,"

he said to the grocer. "I'm a new salesman and wish you would give me some pointers. What do you think I should say to other grocers to sell my soap?"

As he saw the grocer's face soften, he opened the kit again.

"Young feller," the grocer started, and continued for fifteen minutes. Customers waited in the store while the grocer told Wrigley how to sell his soaps. And, of course, as the grocer talked, he sold himself on the soap.

Young Wrigley left with an order for several months' supply of soap—which the grocer had sold himself.

The great sales record of one of our popular-priced automobiles was reached partly because of the instructions that were given all salesmen, time and time again. They were told to ask the customers questions that would make the prospects sell themselves.

When the customers were examining the upholstery the salesman would ask, *not* "Don't you like its feel?" but "What do you like most about the interior of the car?"

The best way to talk a person into cooperating is to let him talk himself into a cooperative mood by asking the right questions.

A group of life insurance underwriters in a Western city of 50,000 decided to pay for an institutional campaign for insurance estates in their local newspapers. They used a full page in each Saturday paper.

Each of the companies represented would gladly have supplied advertisements written by skilled adcraftsmen.

But they decided to use a less professional type of advertisement, and have each one written by an outstanding local citizen.

The citizen's picture was reproduced along with his message exhorting his townspeople to provide for the future. Lawyers, bankers, businessmen, architects, engineers vied with one another, as each poured his heart and soul into the advertisement he wrote.

The insurance men who paid for the expensive campaign say it helped sell only a few small policies, not enough to pay the costs. But they didn't care, for the entire cost, and then some, was borne by the man who wrote the first advertisement in the series.

He was the editor of the newspaper, a man in late middle life. He had owned for years what he thought was a reasonable amount of insurance. But after thinking about insurance as he wrote his advertisement, he went to his underwriter and ordered an additional $100,000 policy.

Many of the other locally important men, who thought they were well insured, also increased their holdings after writing the advertisement—they sold themselves.

Recently I took a trip of several thousand miles into the great northwestern wheat states. I told one group of businessmen about the experiences of Mr. White and others, asking questions to help human relations. The next noon a sales manager for a farm-implement manufacturer asked me to lunch.

"That dope about asking questions seemed so elementary," he said, "that I wondered why a man of your standing would spend so much time on it."

Before I could get uneasy, or ask a question, he smiled. "I changed my mind this forenoon," he went on. "A big rancher came in from about 90 miles east of us. He was madder than hades because priorities kept us from making deliveries when our salesman had promised. He insisted on seeing me and was raising a disturbance in the outer office.

"When he came in, he started giving me 'Hail, Columbia.' He was so cussed abusive, as I guess only a farmer can be, that I began to get mad myself. I was about ready to throw him and his business out of the second-story window, when I suddenly thought of the way that efficiency man got mad at the kid whittling on the stick. So I decided to ask him some innocent questions.

" 'Let's see,' I started in, 'your place is on the north side of the highway, with the cottonwood trees around it, isn't it?'

"Then I got him to tell me how they raised the timbers for his big barn, about his two boys in the army. And when he left, you'd never guess—he'd forgotten all about his peeve and he invited me out for Sunday dinner.

"So your lunch today is on the mad farmer who is treating me to a big meal and is now a cooperative customer, because I took your advice and asked questions when my inclination was to talk back. As I look back now, I've lost a lot of sales, and some employees, because I didn't ask enough sensible questions."

I thought it was the psychological moment to ask a question myself.

"I've to be in North Battleford tomorrow night," I told him. "It is only 110 miles, but it takes ten hours on the accommodation train. I wonder if one of your men is driving that way tomorrow?"

"I have some calls to make up there sometime," he answered, "and might as well go up tomorrow myself."

"But, say," he continued after a thoughtful pause, "What are *you* asking a favor of *me* for? I'm not sore at you!"

Ask people for their opinions, to help their self-confidence.

Ask them for favors, to arouse their cooperativeness.

Answer their question by turning it back to them.

Ask them "and, in addition to that?" to get to the bottom of things.

Try giving orders in the form of questions to keep cooperation.

Make suggestions to the boss in the form of questions.

Ask questions that will let people talk themselves into a cooperative attitude.

3 BE BRIEF
to clear up troubles

Hodge's store was still open at ten o'clock, and I stopped in for some refreshments to take home.

I always find some excuse to stop in at this store, where genial Hubert Hodge has been on the job for more than half a century. He purveys wit and wisdom as well as drugs and sundries.

There is a pay telephone in the front of the store, but, being a Scotchman and a Yankee, I wanted to save a nickel. "May I use your own phone for a local call?" I asked. "I want to see if they need something at home."

"Sure, Donald my boy. It's right back there where we mix prescriptions."

The folks at home did want something, more than I had expected, since company had dropped in.

As Mr. Hodge was giving me the change, an embarrassing thought occurred to me.

"I saved five cents by making a free phone call," I said, "but that free call is costing me $2.40."

He smiled as he clicked the cash register shut.

"Well, when Mr. Barton was teaching me the drug

business fifty years ago," and his entire face was a smile, "one of the first things he taught me was that you can't catch a fish unless you let him open his mouth."

I was reminded of this homely wisdom while sitting in during the discussion of a minor labor dispute. The conference was only making the differences worse. The two groups were getting together like two cats at one dish of milk.

It began to look as though a minor problem might become a major issue, as often happens. Inexperienced men represented the management side of the controversy. They had prepared their case thoroughly and were doing most of the talking. They apparently figured on talking the others into giving up.

The workers, who had the grievances, could scarcely get a word in edgewise. They were eager to tell their story, which they had probably rehearsed the night before. But now they couldn't use it.

Nerves became taut, faces set. Obviously a recess was in order to air the smoke out of the room and to ease the tension.

During the recess I told the foreman and superintendent of my experience with Mr. Hodge's telephone. They laughed, agreeing it was a good joke on me.

"But maybe the joke will be on this meeting," I said. "This conference is bogged down. One of the hardest jobs in human relations is to keep quiet and listen to the other fellow. Those chaps haven't had a chance to talk. They're itching to tell their story. It might be a good idea, when we resume, to try being brief and let the other fellows do most of the talking."

When the meeting resumed the management was brief. The others at last had a chance to talk themselves out. The electric tension cleared. The complaining workers told their story in full, a couple of times at least. They felt much better as soon as they had told it. Management won more by being brief than by trying to monopolize the meeting.

A dignified bishop occupied the section across from me on a recent three-day train ride. Strangely enough, one of his parishioners was on the same train. She was an attractive brunette, returning home at the end of her junior year at college. She was pretty, but some preoccupation made her face dull, expressionless.

The second day out she exposed her problem to the bishop, seeking his sage counsel. I pretended to take a nap, partly to give the girl the impression of privacy she desired but, to be honest, mostly to listen in on something that was none of my business. I was interested to hear a bishop in action outside a pulpit.

The bishop had a stentorian voice. There was no difficulty hearing his private conference above the clatter of the train.

Her parents wanted the girl to stay in college. She wanted to enlist in the woman's auxiliary of the army, right away. Did the bishop think she should heed the call of her parents or of her country? It was a tough spot for the bishop.

What she really wanted to do, as I learned later in

the day, was to tell the bishop how she disagreed violently with her parents' wishes for a social life—she wanted to do something useful, exciting, dramatic. But the bishop did not help her solve her dilemma, because he had a very human failing.

He did the talking.

For an hour and a half he talked against the rattle of the train. He lectured about obligations to one's parents. He preached about the fickleness of college girls' minds. He pictured the temptations of an attractive girl who was surrounded by soldiers.

Poor girl! She hardly got in a word edgeways. The bishop was wound up. And he left the girl more perplexed than ever, for she had not had a chance to unburden herself.

It was fate that crowded the dining car that evening, so that the steward had to seat me at a small table, opposite her. She gave a hasty look of recognition at my whiskers and continued nibbling her salad. I did not wish a worried, silent dinner companion, so I practiced asking questions and being brief.

I asked about the class pin she wore, and she told me about her college. Yes, she had just completed a course with Professor Blank, a friend of mine at her college.

Her face brightened. She was talking now, about things in which she was interested. She had an audience—of one —listening intently. She had wanted to talk for days.

Then I told her, briefly, of the high regard my son had for the young women who do ground-crew work in the Royal Air Force, how he had joined the force unbeknown to me, but how proud I had been of him. There was a natural temptation to show his picture and tell her about some of his ferry and bombing experiences, but, *no*, be brief, Laird—let the other person talk.

When I mentioned women in the service her face clouded momentarily. We were both silent for what seemed a long time. Then she began to talk about her problems, hesitatingly at first, then eagerly, with a rush of words. She told me, a stranger, what she had wanted to tell her bishop. But now she had a listener who was being brief—friendly, but brief.

She told about her sweetheart, an engineering student, now a prisoner of war in Hong Kong and his fate unknown. She had not told the bishop this, yet it was the reason for her keen desire to enter the service herself. There is no arguing with an impelling reason like that.

She told the stranger the problem she had with her parents.

I listened through a second pot of tea. She became radiant as she talked on and on. The clouds lifted from her face. It was a beauty treatment, just to have someone listen for once.

I knew she had reached a decision but did not ask what it was. Yet I feel certain what she decided and admire her for it.

Her decision was not my concern. But I was glad to help a distraught girl find peace within herself. The best way is to be brief and to listen. It is a temptation to give vent to one's own opinion and consider the matter settled. That never settles it.

In Chapter 19 of *Practical Business Psychology* you can learn more about clearing up others' troubles.

Edgar was born with a silver spoon in his mouth, but he survived the handicap. He inherited control of a large factory before he was thirty. It was a man-sized burden, and he carried it like a man. Things went along beautifully until employees and townspeople, in a burst of enthusiasm, elected him burgess of the small Pennsylvania city.

The first Friday in each month, grievance day was held in the city hall. It was then that taxpayers spouted about their troubles to the burgess. The foreign-born even brought their home troubles, complaints about a husband's infidelity, for instance, which were not exactly city business.

It was these Friday night "blowoff" sessions that made Edgar haggard. As a conscientious young man he tried to placate each complainer by giving the city's side of the case. That merely made the complainers shout more loudly or give forth personal invective. Thus Edgar was thoroughly, but unintentionally, arguing each one into a worse frame of mind. The complainers left, unsatisfied, sore at the burgess. They began to turn against the factory, too.

Edgar realized this was harmful for the business and for his family. He could think of no way out except to resign his public office. But one Friday night he accidentally discovered a way out.

He was particularly tired, and the stuffy air and glaring light of the hearing room made him drowsy. A foreign woman, shawl over her head, was voicing her complaints. She was difficult to understand. As she talked she became excited and talked so rapidly as to be unintelligible. Edgar did not stop her. He had gone to sleep in his chair. Fortunately the woman did not notice the burgess was asleep, but others did and hid grins behind their hands.

When Edgar awakened, he pulled himself together and started to clear his throat.

"Oh! Thank you! Thank you!" she said, bowing almost to the floor in front of him. "You are a good burgess. You have help me."

No one knew what her complaint had been. But Edgar won the decision by sleeping through it. He had been unusually brief, and she had talked herself out of the argument.

For the balance of that term, and his next two terms, he just sat solemn on these once-dreaded Friday nights, and let the complainers talk themselves out.

His amusing experience taught him that we can often win an argument by being brief, and listening.

During the Second World War, Edgar was assigned to handle the troublesome problem of helping small manufacturers who did not have facilities for war production and who might be forced out of business. This

was a job that could have plenty of headaches for everyone concerned.

But he remembered the lesson of his nap that amusing
Friday night.

The small-manufacturer situation in Edgar's zone was
handled with fewer headaches than anywhere else in the
country. You probably saw his picture in the newspapers
and trade journals and read the words of praise his accomplishments merited.

When I saw it, I thought of the old lady with her shawl
—and Edgar asleep.

That sleep woke him up to the importance of being
brief, and listening, when leading people.

Be brief in striking a bargain, too. Accidents have
taught many the dollars-and-cents value of brevity when
a deal is being made. Gracie Allen and George Burns, for
instance. They were a moderately well paid vaudeville
team when they appeared as guest stars on a radio program.

They were an instant hit, and a talent scout wanted to
sign them up at once. He offered them $750 to appear
on another radio program. That sum left Burns and Allen
speechless. Burns gulped, stared at the scout, and said,
"How much?" He could scarcely believe his ears and
could think of nothing more to say.

"Oh, well," said the scout, "we can do better—but not
a cent more than $1,000."

Remember that when you ask the boss for a raise.

Samson killed ten thousand with the jawbone of an ass.

Today many talk themselves out of promotions with the same weapon.

Be brief in conversation. Keep your stories short; don't drag them out. Skip a lot of the details you might want to include. Make each a short short story. It is the timing —coming to the punch, or the end, quickly and almost unexpectedly—that keeps people interested.

If you cannot interest others in what you say, you may be fairly certain that you are taking too long to say it. Make it brisk, not long-winded. Most of us are more long-winded than we realize. I had to learn this the hard way. Now I don't bore audiences because I have notes for many more things than I can possibly say in the time allotted. So I have to breeze through the meat of the talk and have no time to pick daisies by the wayside.

Being brief keeps conversation interesting. If you want the minute details, read a book.

I was talking with a magazine editor about an idea for an article. He was definitely interested.

"How long would you make it," he asked me, "and how much would it be worth?"

"About 3,000 words would be adequate to tell the story," I said, and mentioned what I thought was a fair price.

"Boil it down to 1,000 words—and we'll pay you twice that figure," was his instant reply.

There is apparently a dollars-and-cents value in brevity.

THE NEW STYLE

Business and social groups are getting an increasing share of new-style leaders. These trained leaders are displacing the old-style, who elbowed their

Old · style bosses (Autocratic)

Knew it all; made decisions himself, then pushed to make the decisions workable.

Talked aggressively. Tried to get people to follow him by talking or arguing them into it.

Felt that good pay for an honest day's work was enough for anyone.

Kept others in the dark about future plans or proposed changes. Did the planning himself. "I."

Tried to control others by having strict rules and giving orders. Discipline and penalties.

Kept his distance, so they would respect him and obey when he spoke.

Policy of finding fault on theory they would work harder, or not ask for a raise. Put on pressure.

Felt that the attitudes, ideals, goals he told them to have were what they would have.

Acted on theory that success of an undertaking depended on the judgment and hard work of a few gifted people (such as himself). "My goal."

44

*way up by "doing what came naturally"
in handling people. This comparative
listing shows some of the basic differences in the two styles.*

New · style leaders (Democratic)

Feels his way. Asks questions; gets help from those concerned
as he reaches decisions.

Brief in talking. Listens to learn what others think, or know,
or feel, and leads through their own ideas.

Adds a "mental wage" of congenial work groups and a feeling of being appreciated.

Keeps members of social or work group up to date on what
may be in store; often works out plans with them.
"We."

Not much dependence on rules and penalties; more freedom
of discussion to bring out the best in others.

Acts as human as the next one. Closer to the group, and they
follow him for other reasons than his authority or
wealth.

More use of encouragement and helping others solve their
business and social problems. Eases frustrations.

Realizes such thinking is picked up from work
crews and other groups they belong to,
so leads through these rather than by
"preaching."

Methods based on belief an organization suc-
ceeds by teamwork, people pulling together all up and down the line. "Our
goal."

45

A famous redheaded actress missed a chance for a brilliant marriage because she was not brief. Her suitor, now an outstanding sculptor, went on a picnic with her. His main purpose was privacy, as he was all set to propose.

But the redhead was wound up. She kept "upstage" all afternoon, and talked and talked. Actually, he did not get a chance to propose. After listening to her monologue, he began to wonder about the wisdom of marrying her anyway.

They have lived happily ever after, but not together.

I wonder how many have talked themselves out of a proposal?

It was an unhappily married man, I am sure, who said the sculptor might as well have married the actress, as the picnic afternoon was a sample of any married life.

Being brief and listening are as useful after marriage as during courtship. The trick is to see that each does his fair share of listening as well as of talking.

Half a dozen top-flight corporation executives at the Union League Club were discussing the apparent dearth of young men capable of taking on higher responsibilities with their firms. They agreed that there was no shortage of men with intelligence, who knew details of the businesses, who had sound ideas.

Their problem was to discover men they could trust, men who did not talk too much. Too much talking gives away business secrets, jams deals.

This is what Einstein had in mind when he gave the formula for success as

$$x + y + z = success$$

He said that x represented hard work, y represented play. Someone asked him what the z stood for.

"That," said the genius, "is the ability to keep your mouth shut."

We learn by listening, not by talking.

When we are brief and listen, we bolster the other person's ego.

When a situation is tense, listen.

When someone is angry, be brief, let him talk.

When someone is unhappy, be brief and listen.

4 CONFIDENT BEARING
to help control others

While still a youngster in grade school, I worked one summer in Harvey Morley's print shop. About eight-thirty Saturday night my first week's work was finished, and I was paid off in hard cash. It was good money, though there was not much of it—fifty cents.

As I started homeward across the public square of the Indiana town, I saw a crowd gathered around a gas-lit wagon. I joined the crowd, elbowing my way to the edge of the platform on the back of the wagon.

A medicine man was extolling the healing virtues of his sirup. He talked rapidly, seriously. He was confident of his product. All human ailments were helped by the mystic Aztec formula he claimed to have discovered in some Mexican excavations—so he said. He had Mexican souvenirs on the platform, and I never once doubted any of his claims.

But I was in terribly robust health, without a pain or ache. So I started to leave. The "professor" pointed his finger at me.

"Look at this lad," he shouted to the audience. "The bloom of health is on his cheeks. I had a son like that myself. And then—then, one sad day he was suddenly stricken and taken away from me. Oh! my friends! Oh! If I had only known in those dark hours about this Aztec remedy!"

I stopped and gulped. I concentrated on finding a sick feeling somewhere, but located none. Good health plagued me. Yet this man was so confident of the universal need for his concoction that I couldn't pass up the opportunity of a lifetime. Anyway, I had my first earned half dollar burning a hole through my pocket.

When he announced the price of his medicine, my heart sank; it was a dollar a bottle. But he hurriedly continued—since he was a native Hoosier himself, he would let us buy a bottle of the medicine, a tin of ointment, and his own almanac and crop forecaster, the whole lot for the ridiculous price of 50 cents. Not only that, but the first ten customers would get a photograph of him and his curios.

It took a week's wages, but I bought the assortment, including the picture. Before I was home, I wondered why I had bought the stuff. I kept it hidden for some time and finally threw it out, along with the photograph.

The professor and explorer was undoubtedly a great liar. His dopes were likely worthless. It was not just small boys who were suckers for him. Mature men—including the mayor—bought his assortment. I was in good company.

I was not a sucker because I was a small boy, but because I was as human as the others, even the mayor.

The medicine man's secret was his confident manner.

A confident manner does things to people, to the one who assumes the confident manner as well as to those around him.

Hesitation or timidity does things to people, too; it holds many back. Call it ingrown modesty, if you wish, but it would smell the same by any name.

Many nitwits and incompetents get farther in the world than they should, because they have heaps of confidence—or perhaps just a knack for bluffing confidence. Sooner or later they get beyond their depth. You know this type—the happy-go-lucky chap who lands good jobs, but can't hold them; the woman who organizes some activity but can't keep it running after it is started.

These people who have risen higher than their brain power warrants, merely because they had unjustifiable confidence, used to annoy me, but no longer. I just wait for the false front to wear off as their mediocre ability comes through the surface.

But it is heartbreaking to know people with real ability who are held down because they have not learned the lesson of putting on a confident manner. I now deliberately try to get such people mad, for a reason you will soon understand; perhaps you will get mad, too—at yourself.

A skeptical acquaintance in the southland thought I overrated the need for a confident manner. He went out to test it.

A Metropolitan Opera star was singing in Atlanta's

largest theater. Lee put on a tuxedo, went to the theater, and lounged around the stage door for a few minutes. He flicked his cigarette into the street and turned to the grizzled guard at the stage door.

"Looks like a good crowd tonight," Lee said as he walked in.

"We always get a good house for a star like your man, sir," the doorkeeper replied, touching the brim of his hat.

An assumed confident manner had worked well so far. But inside it might be different, for the next quarry was the great star himself! He was standing on the distant side of the stage.

Lee did not hesitate. He saw a small parcel, picked it up, and rushed to the famous baritone.

"Is everything going all right?" Lee asked as he shook hands. They chatted a few minutes. Then Lee handed him the package and did not ask, but said confidently, "Hold this for me awhile," and he left. As far as he knows the singer may still be holding that package!

In serious situations an assumed confident manner works just as well. It has helped weather many a crisis. It helped George Westinghouse hold his young company together in the panic of 1907. Receivership was waiting around the corner for the company, but it could pull through if the workers stuck by.

So Westinghouse began to talk enthusiastically to his men about new machines they could make. He showed sketches and models, painted word pictures of the profits in the new ideas. This was done as much to make himself feel confident during the hard times as it was to influence others, but it did influence others. His employees caught his confidence and from their savings accounts took out enough money to tide the company through the crisis.

Remember that whenever you see the name Westinghouse on a product or in an advertisement. It would not be a familiar name now if Westinghouse had not assumed a confident manner back in 1907.

When John D. Rockefeller was thirty-five years old a confident manner helped him expand his business on a shoestring. He had more assumed confidence than cash in those days, yet he bought up competitor after competitor. When the price was agreed upon, he would take out his checkbook.

"Shall I write a check, or do you prefer payment in Standard Oil stock?" he asked them.

Invariably, they took the shares of stock and, incidentally, made themselves richer by so doing—something to think of the next time you are admiring the magnitude of Rockefeller Center in New York.

An assumed confident manner helped a young Tennessee bank cashier. Seventeen Chattanooga banks had closed, and a line of depositors began to form at Tom Preston's suburban bank. They wanted their money before his small bank closed, too.

Preston's bank was in sound condition, but it did not have ready cash to pay off all the agitated depositors. So twenty-five-year-old Preston used the secret of a confident manner. Most of the depositors wanted to take out only a portion of their deposits, but Preston insisted that they take out all or none—he said he didn't want customers who had only 40 or 50 per cent confidence in the bank.

One big depositor thought Preston was bluffing but changed his mind when given a load of $16,000 in small bills to lug home. The cashier's confident manner as he stacked up the money did something to the depositor. He put the cash back on deposit and told the others who were in line they were fools to take their money out. The run was over!

I wish you could know Major Harry Hurd. He is one of the most admirable men I have ever met and he has a powerful way with him.

He has had only two years of schooling in his entire life, yet he is an inspiring public speaker and a leading citizen wherever he is located. He went to work when he was a lad of ten and has worked steadily for nearly sixty years.

His work nowadays requires the highest kind of leadership—he takes money away from people, for a cause.

When a Community Chest drive bogs down somewhere, Major Harry is sent for. When a new hospital is needed, the doughty little major is asked to raise the money.

As a boy he went to work on the docks. Towering above the same docks now is a gigantic hospital, built with funds that he raised after highly educated people had failed at the job.

One evening I asked him what one thing, more than any other, made him so successful in raising millions of dollars. He did not hesitate. The major never hesitates, for he is a man with a swift and confident manner.

"When I was carrying coal and potatoes on the docks," he said, "I learned how to swear. That has been a handicap, a habit hard to break.

"But I also learned that I had the best results from others if I acted as though it were impossible for me to fail. I just take it for granted that the other fellow will do what I want. That has been an asset—and it was an easy habit to acquire.

"It makes me forget my lack of education when I call on a university president and give him the names of ten men from whom we expect him to collect $5,000 apiece.

"I never ask people if they will do it, I just confidently assume they will and thank them in advance.

"I've learned never to infect people with a doubt. Doubts never paid off debts. Doubts never get people to work with you wholeheartedly."

Luck has helped some people catch on to this secret for themselves. Walter told me recently, for example, how he got his first big promotion. He was foreman in a Cleveland metalworking factory. Business was booming and the firm was starting a branch plant downstate. Some lucky foreman in the Cleveland shop would be assistant superintendent in the new plant. Walter did not think he was in line for the promotion.

On his way to work one morning a traffic cop called him down. Walter was still boiling mad at the cop when he reached the shop.

He threw his coat over the back of his chair and started working with a zip. The general manager chose that particular morning to walk into Walter's cubicle. A few days later Walter was called to the big office upstairs.

"We have gone over the records of each foreman with a fine-tooth comb," he was told. "On paper, you all look good. But when I visited you the other morning, you had a forcefulness and a confidence that make me think you could swing the job at the new plant better than any of the men. The superintendent's job will not be easy. He will need the strength that confidence gives in order to control others."

Walter chuckled as he related this. "To think," he added, "that I got the job because I was sore at a cop, and the boss thought it was confidence and fight.

"But it made me think. A false show of confidence got me the boost, so I decided that if I was going to make good, I'd better show some real confidence. At the time, I didn't have an average dose of it. But I realized I had to have it, so I just made some for myself and have been using it ever since."

After he got his pipe going he continued. "I never did see that cop again, but I've always wanted to, for I owe him a box of cigars for making me mad that morning."

We don't need to get mad at someone else to have the

determined manner that suggests confidence and begets confidence itself. After we have assumed the manner for a while, it becomes a part of us.

We can simply get mad at ourselves for not showing it.

An immigrant became assistant foreman in a large Buffalo plant. He would have become a foreman, but he fell victim to arthritis. Finally he was confined to bed, apparently helpless. The oldest son left college and went to work with a newspaper to help support the family. All the family plans for the future had to be canceled. The cripple felt hopeless as well as helpless. Gloom pervaded the family and interfered with their work.

A physician called a couple of times a week, but left no confidence.

One day the oldest son took matters in his own hands and brought in another physician.

"Your father has been receiving the right medicines," he said, "except one priceless ingredient. He has been given vitamins and serums, but what he needs most is an injection of hope. He will never be better physically, but he can have more confidence for his future.

"I am going to continue the same medicines but I'll have them made up in different colors so he will think they are different. And I am going to give him the real medicine he needs in the form of little white lies—and you must help me. You have to take the long faces off the relatives."

The next day the young physician breezed into the sickroom. "Let's see you wiggle your fingers, Pop," he

MEMORIZED BETTER WHEN THEY FELT CONFIDENT

Memory score:

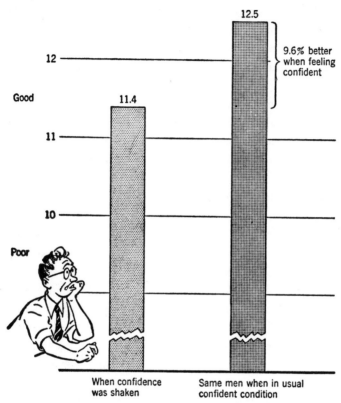

12.5

9.6% better
when feeling
confident

12 ──────────────

Good   11.4

11 ──────────────

10 ──────────────

Poor

When confidence   Same men when in usual
was shaken   confident condition

Memorizing long numbers similar to telephone numbers was tested in 16 men. Later in the test their confidence was shaken by telling them there was something peculiar about their memory. Many other tests confirm these results which show how feeling confident helps one use one's abilities. This experiment with numbers was by Dr. and Mrs. Stanley Moldawsky.

57

said. "Fine, fine," he lied, for they would never be more flexible.

"Pretty soon you can be using them," he went on. "What hobbies did you used to have, Pop?"

He had once liked to tinker with watches. Good! Get a tilt-top table beside the bed and get ready to go into the neighborhood watch-repair business. That is what Pop is doing now. He tasted the medicine of feeling confident about the future, and now confidence is his. He makes a comfortable living, confined to his bed, repairing watches. Confidence kept him off the human junk pile.

Confidence is a good medicine.

Back in college I earned room and board for a couple of years serving as janitor in a home for old women. Poor old Grandma Ruff used to have spells when she could not sleep. When insomnia got the best of her she would totter down the hall to the matron's room for a sleeping pill.

One sleepless night she turned the wrong way in the corridor and ended up at my room, asking for a sleeping pill. I knew nothing about sleeping pills but suspected the value of a confident manner. I pulled on a robe and went to the kitchen, where I found a large, dry navy bean.

I gave her this bean in the dimly lit corridor. "This is bigger and more powerful than the ones you have been getting," I lied to her, "so hurry to bed before you go to sleep standing up."

From that prankish night on, Grandma Ruff always insisted on having the big, strong sleep pills the young fellow gave her. They worked so much better than the ones that really had chemical powers to bring sleep!

Confidence is indeed good medicine.

Watch your letters and reports, too. They should keep a tone of confidence. Don't follow the mimeographed letter I received last week from a professional psychologist, who should have known better. "Few members seem interested," the letter concluded. So, naturally, I did not attend the meeting, either.

A young architect had been able to land only the lowest job with a firm of architects. With the decline in building he lost that and could not land another. He had used his last dime for bus fare to hunt for a job. He needed money to get home and stopped at a pawnbroker's to pawn a $1.50 watch.

He asked for a loan of only 10 cents on the watch, just enough for bus fare. After three pawnbrokers had turned him down he was thoroughly disgusted by their indifference, mad at himself over his plight.

So it was a changed man who entered the fourth shop with the $1.50 watch. He was in desperation, not whining, but determined. He pushed his watch into the broker's gnarled hand and said, "Give me a dollar on that."

"Not a penny more than 50 cents," the broker replied as he started to fill out the receipts.

Appear confident, not only in your words, but also in the firmness in which they are said.

Have a confident handshake.

Put on leather heels to make your step sound confident—English soldiers have metal taps on their shoes to give a confident sound to the tread of their feet.

Approach others with shoulders back, head up, chin forward, confident in every sinew. Stand tall, always.

Remember these eight words: "Act as if it were impossible to fail!"

5 DIRECTNESS
to make personal contact

A roly-poly Colorado girl made a fool out of me during my third year of high school. She didn't do it on purpose. Come to think it over, she didn't make a fool out of me —I did it myself.

I was daffy about her. Apparently she did not know I existed.

So I tried dressing for her special benefit. I was bound to have her notice me, and favorably. One Sunday afternoon I borrowed a pair of white trousers from Harry Magee. He was considerably shorter than I, so I turned the cuffs down. I traded two somber neckties for one with brilliant yellow and red stripes. Most of the afternoon I lounged in this attention-demanding outfit across from the girl's dormitory. But Florence did not pass by. On Monday I learned she had spent the week end in Des Moines.

Then I tried music. I sent to Chicago for their cheapest mail-order instrument, and a book of teach-yourself-at-home lessons. She had to pass my window three afternoons a week on her way to the gym. At those times I would stand hopefully in the wide-open window, regardless of the weather, and blow my loudest and sweetest when I saw her coming. Apparently she was hard of hearing, and it was a long time before I liked music again.

That winter she was interested in our basketball star. By spring I decided to give him competition and perhaps get some notice from Florence. I quit my surreptitious smoking and went into training for cross-country running. I ran to meals, to classes, to take care of the furnaces, to church. If motion caught attention, I should have had it. But the nearest I came to getting notice from her was one afternoon when her botany class was meeting outdoors.

I hastily put on my running togs and trotted around and around the class until the instructor asked me please to go somewhere else.

It was not entirely accidental that, twenty years later, I saw Florence in Nebraska. The once roly-poly girl now had a touch of middle-aged spread. But there were the same smile and giggle and red-tinted curls.

We talked about our families, laughed about the old high-school days. She remembered how I ran circles around that botany class and said she was furious at the instructor for reprimanding me. This brought a flush of sedate middle-aged embarrassment to my face.

She had actually noticed my adolescent antics! But yet I did not seem to make any impression on her in those days or attract her attention. Why? Now I could safely ask, and it was her turn to blush.

She said I never seemed to notice her, so there.

Never noticed her! Why, I noticed her so much I made myself ridiculous, but I had made the blunder of trying to attract attention instead of giving it.

When I said, "Hello," I had talked right past her. When she looked at me, I had glanced shyly to one side. I had been so self-conscious I acted half conscious.

Notice others—and let them know it by directness.

I had been like one of my first bosses. When he gave orders, no one in the gang knew to whom he was directing them. He talked right past us, out of the window or down the shop.

The result was confusion confounded. Either none of us or all of us tried to carry out the order. Usually it was no one, for we naturally passed the buck and assumed the order was for the other fellow, especially if it was unpleasant. We had perfect alibis for stalling.

One afternoon he shouted something about grinding off nibs in a hurry to five of us who were working in the corner. Chopper, who stammered, was easily excited.

"Wh-wh-wh-WHO? M-m-m-m-mm-mE?" Chopper exclaimed.

Months of resentment over the boss's indirect, impersonal approach to us made us break out in furious laughter at Chopper's startled exclamation. It became a standing joke with us. After that, when the chief issued orders into space, rather than to us directly, the squad would shout, as one man, "Wh-wh-who? M-m-m-me?"

We broke him of the habit in a month. Insubordination, perhaps, but it was enjoyable horseplay and made a better leader of him.

It taught him not to ignore people but to talk directly to them.

One of the biggest disappointments in my life, much greater, honestly, than being ignored by Florence (I found another roly-poly girl!), occurred when I first went to graduate school. I had chosen this school primarily because of an internationally famed scientist who taught there. For the first month a fussy old maid taught the course for him. Then came the day when the great professor himself appeared.

There was an awed hush in the room. He adjusted his half-moon spectacles, cleared his throat. We were on the edges of the seats, but he looked out the window.

He thumped a pack of dog-eared file cards together on the desk. Maybe he was going to play solitaire? Apparently he was unaware of us—admirers from afar who thrilled at being so close to him.

He cleared his throat again and started to talk—from the file cards and right to them. Maybe he couldn't see us through those half-glasses?

But wait! Now he was looking at us—no, over us, at the ceiling. He asked a question no one could answer, chuckled at our ignorance, then went back to talking to his fistful of file cards.

Most people felt he was intentionally ignoring them, so they ignored him, too. Some said he seemed to live in a remote world. The more caustic said he was just a laboratory machine, not a human being.

But he was human and generous and helpful. He was

unhappy because people did not warm up to him. He had power over others through his brilliant brains, his position, his reputation, but he lacked the power that really stirs people and touches off a loyal enthusiasm. He did not make the contact that reaches into people's minds.

If unhappy Professor Fritz had only been direct, had only looked at people, had only talked to them instead of past them, his influence would have been much greater. If he had been direct, he would have gained the contact with others he craved, the contact any leader needs to reach into people, to be more than a machine issuing wisdom or orders.

Let people know you are interested in *them* by looking directly at them, talking directly to them.

Look at them intently when they are talking to you.

Edouard inherited considerable responsibility with the family firm. He had a good head and went through the graduate school of business to train himself for carrying on the family trade.

At my first meeting with him I noticed he was not direct; he talked to my watch chain or at a safety chart on his office wall. I thought he might be ill at ease, but even after we became well acquainted his indirectness persisted. His subordinates complained that he had always been that way. They thought it showed he did not like them.

His doting mother was rather proud of Edouard's indirectness. She said it showed he was modest. She thought the organization was not holding together well because the others resented the wealth and power Edouard had inherited.

They resented more the impression of aloofness that his indirect glance and talk suggested. They assumed he felt superior or wanted to ignore them.

The tough problem was how to bring this home to Edouard convincingly but in a way that would not offend him. Then we found a way.

Edouard thought Franklin D. Roosevelt was a great natural leader who would go far. But he thought Herbert Hoover had a better grasp of world problems. He considered it a pity that more people did not follow Hoover. Here was the solution of my problem. The evening before I had seen a newsreel in which both Roosevelt and Hoover said a few words. I attended it again, this time with Edouard.

"Did the President seem to look at you?" I asked afterward.

"He talked right to me," Edouard said. "This may sound impossible, but he seemed to be ignoring everybody else and to be looking at and talking just to me."

"And the former president?" I asked, getting closer to my point.

"Now that you mention it," he replied, "Hoover seemed to be talking to someone in the left side of the balcony, like this."

I waited for Edouard to continue. He was still looking into the imaginary balcony.

"Say," he exclaimed, turning his eyes directly to mine

for the first time, "I think I know why you wanted me to see that newsreel. I've been talking to the left side of the balcony. I've been thinking more about what I was saying than about the person to whom I was talking. Smart idea to see that newsreel!"

The newsreel demonstration worked wonders with Edouard's leadership. It did not improve his knowledge of the business, but it did give him a better understanding of the business of reaching into people's minds by being direct.

Now he thinks first about the people to whom he is talking and secondly about what he is saying. He talks directly to them and, whether he is talking or listening to them, looks directly at them.

At a company dinner some time later I sat beside the treasurer. He preferred to look at pages of figures rather than at people. He looked at the emblem in my coat lapel and said confidently to it:

"This war work has certainly made a new man of Edouard. Not a person in the organization now but does cheerfully things they used to do reluctantly for him. The transformation is amazing. And he'll make a lot better president for the company than his father was, and the old man was dynamite."

I nodded in agreement. "It is astonishing," I said, "how people seem to have added strength when they look others in the eye."

His glance shifted from my lapel to the bridge of my nose. "I think I get your point," he said.

Did you ever see a man closing a million-dollar sale against the best competition in the country? I did, and I found what made him one of the top advertising salesmen. Other men from the big agency had worked on this fat account; they had wined and dined the prospect but they couldn't get the pen on the dotted line.

Then Jack went after it single-handed. His total entertainment expense was 20 cents for cigars. I was in Jack's office when he showed the prospect proposed drawings and layouts for the advertising. The desk was cluttered with these and with lists of magazines in which he recommended they advertise.

Jack picked up one of the proposed advertisements; then he explained it, talking right to the doubting prospect, not to the "ad." He laid that "ad" down and picked up the next one, without taking his eyes from Mr. Million Dollar Prospect.

But the pixies had done something to the stack of "ads." Jack picked up the wrong "ad." He didn't take his eyes off the prospect but talked earnestly about the "ad" he imagined he was holding.

It was amusing. I grinned, but Jack and Mr. Prospect did not, for neither of them had noticed the error. That direct gaze and direct talk of Jack's were almost hypnotic. The prospect did not notice the ads and he was oblivious of my presence. Directness had reached into his mind, and he was in Jack's power.

You salesmen, remember that. Talk to the prospect. Don't talk to the policy or product. It's the customer you have to reach.

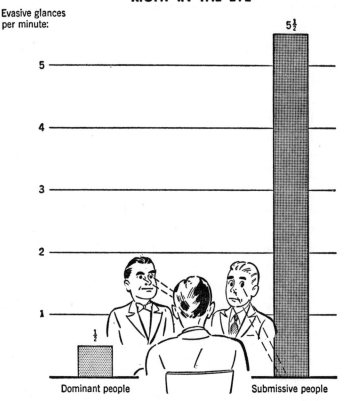

THE DOMINANT PEOPLE LOOKED THEM RIGHT IN THE EYE

Evasive glances
per minute:

People known to be submissive were compared with others known to be dominant. During this test each did simple mental arithmetic while looking another person in the eye. The submissive people shifted their glance away from the other person 11 times as often as did the dominant people. From experiments by Drs. Henry T. Moore and Adam R. Gilliland.

69

And beware of your canned sales talk. It is poison if you reel it off blankly from memory. Tell it to the prospect, not to the room in general.

Two don't's:
1. Don't try to outstare the other person. Look at his chin or the tip of his nose. Talk to his mouth.
2. Don't get too close. Two feet away is close enough for most people, and too close for some. Arm's length is a safe all-round distance. Remember that, after they are forty years old, most people see best at arm's length and need special glasses to see at closer distances.

And a very special do for married folks:
Do look directly at your wife at least a time or two during the meal. You would be astonished to know how much of your looking has been into the plate.

And when she asks how you like her new hat, for heaven's sake look directly at it, then at her, and tell your prettiest lie.

And if she doesn't cook something especially nice for the next meal, it's because you told that white lie to the floor or to the ceiling.

We can't even tell a lie successfully unless we are direct about it!

General Barton K. Yount, in charge of flight training in the Second World War, stepped out of his plane at a field where his son was in training. A long line of dignitaries met him as he emerged from the plane, and General Yount passed down the line, shaking hands with each. At the end of the line he paused, asked, "Where's Bart?"

"You just shook hands with him, General," he was told.

"Damnedest thing that could happen to a father," he exclaimed. "That will teach me to look a man in the face when I shake his hand!"

6

EARNESTNESS
to arouse enthusiasm

Seth developed leadership speedily, just as he lost it overnight years before. His regained leadership improved the
lives of several hundred people in one of those placid New
England villages built around a white church and a green.
A new sincerity did it.

Seth had been puttering around most of his fifty-odd
years, pretending to run the little factory around which
the village revolved.

It was a typical small plant—a tall chimney surrounded
by a dozen antiquated punch presses and rows of greasy
assembly benches. The adjacent pond had been made
years before by Seth's grandfather for water power. In
every direction there were beautiful rolling hills—and
inside the factory the grime of years.

Seth had not worked hard at running the business. He
was not exactly a loafer but certainly was not a hustler.
He kept busy, but halfheartedly. The plant had been
slack for years, but folks didn't complain much; it gave
some work, which was better than nothing. Folks felt
sorry for Seth, anyway.

It was an open secret that Seth had little use for the

factory's products. "Junk" was what he called the novelties his plant stamped out by the thousands. Workers and townspeople agreed with him, but it gave them a meager living.

Like Seth, his employees were working in low gear and not interested in bettering their lot. It was a sorrowfully dispirited community, as so many small villages are.

It had not always been so. Years before, as a young man, Seth had made a whirlwind start with the plant. He made the village hum, but for only a few years. Older residents say that Seth changed overnight early in the First World War. He had been elated over the birth of his first child, a son. Four days later he was filled with despair at the sudden death of his wife.

He never got back his former zest and spark. He just did what had to be done, and his neighbors seemed to understand.

An unmarried sister came to keep house for him and help raise the boy. Father and son became close companions, sharing the affection that would have been the mother's.

When the Second World War broke out, the boy had finished engineering school and was starting to work with his father. The lad was cut out for factory work but was restless. He sometimes shuddered when he contrasted the dirt, disorder, and thumping of the punch presses with the beautiful hills that could be seen dimly through the dusty windows.

"The whole world will be as cheerless as that factory," he said to his father one evening, "unless we can stop the Nazis. They will make the world worse than those damned presses. I'm not doing much to help out here."

Seth knew what the boy was thinking and reluctantly watched him go off on active duty a few days later. The boy had had a second lieutenant's training at college.

It was soon almost impossible for the plant to get metal for its novelties. Seth agreed with Washington that his products were not a necessity—just junk. He thought about munitions production but figured that this was out of the question with his antiquated equipment. Business almost stopped.

He was standing at the windows one day, watching the clouds above the snow-covered hills, wondering where his son would spend Christmas. He had ceased to wonder about the plant.

The railroad station agent came in, cap in hand, with a telegram. Martin usually phoned the messages, but Seth thought the agent dropped in on his way for a morning cup of coffee.

As Seth opened the wire he knew why Martin had carried it down through the snow: "The War Department regrets to inform you that your son is missing as a result of an engagement with the enemy in the performance of his duty in the service of his country."

Seth stayed for a long time alone in his office, intent upon the hills and clouds. At noon he told his office-girl-of-all-work that he was going to Boston for a few days. Sincerity of purpose was starting.

At Boston he went directly to the regional procurement office and looked carefully through mimeographed specification and bid sheets for war orders. Why, here were some washers the country needs, and he could make those on his punch presses! He found other bits and pieces he could make, too.

Seth hurried back to his village. People greeted him with solemn faces. But it was a new Seth, with a determined expression. He got his Yankee ingenuity out of storage and found his plant could make many war materials.

The place began to hum. The workers quickly caught Seth's spirit, and the old benches and presses had to take it. Seth had a firmer set around his jaw, and his employees were holding their heads higher.

Seth also stepped in and steamed up the slow-moving village defense organization. Previously he had attended to his own business and taken no hand in community efforts. Now he was the mainspring in the village. Now he was working, for the first time in years, with grim earnestness.

The cruel fate of missing men had unloosed an unconquerable spirit that Seth had been burying under the junk in his plant. At last he was sold on the usefulness of his work—bits and pieces, but they could save other fathers' sons.

This newborn earnestness made Seth the leader he might have been years before.

This earnestness—a sincere faith in the importance of one's task—is a priceless ingredient among the qualities of leadership.

It gave Seth a dynamic quality. It touched off the best efforts of others. It aroused their enthusiasm, for Seth was enthusiastic now.

There is no leadership without sincerity, courage, and an enthusiasm that springs from earnestness.

It is said that a person must be willing to accept responsibility if he is to become a leader. The person with earnestness does more than accept responsibility—he seeks it.

It is a dangerous thing, this earnestness. Cranks and crackpots usually have an abnormal amount of earnestness. So do fanatical religious organizers, proponents of erratic economic schemes, instigators of labor troubles.

In contrast, the average citizen plods along his sensible, matter-of-fact way, without earnestness and without exerting much influence.

The fire of earnestness spreads rapidly; cults and embattled groups spring up around earnest but eccentric people. Foolish men who have the fire of earnestness can lead, while levelheaded men who work halfheartedly cannot.

Disappointment is the lot of those who try to lead by logic alone. Many take night and correspondence courses to get more into their heads; but to lead, they need something in their hearts, too. They must be enthusiastic for their work, their company, their products, their associates, their future.

There is no leadership without earnestness.

Frederick's father had been the town drunkard and years ago he mysteriously disappeared. To this day no one knows what happened to him.

So young Fred had to go to work early in life, at hard physical work. At twenty-five he was disabled in an accident and had to quit his job. He gradually drifted into selling life insurance but did not sell much.

Then his sister's husband was killed in the railroad yards. A few years before Fred had sold him a small policy. That kept Fred's sister from going through the hardships that, he remembered all too clearly, his mother had suffered after his father disappeared.

Up to that time Fred had been selling life insurance to make a living, but his brother-in-law's death made him begin to sell with earnestness. He no longer sold to make money but to bring help.

When a prospect was not interested, Fred would say brusquely, "If you were my own brother, I'd grab you by the neck and drag you to the medical examiner."

There was nothing tactful about that, but the earnestness did something to cynical prospects. More and more bought.

"If you were my own brother" was not an idle phrase. It expressed Fred's sincere feelings. It means more to the prospects than tables of rates and cash values. His attitude of earnestness, not his knowledge of insurance laws, sold his policies.

For many years Fred sold more than a million dollars' worth of insurance year after year. He became one of the country's big producers because of his earnestness.

Remember that magic phrase, *If you were my own brother*, when you want to arouse enthusiasm.

You don't need to say the phrase, just act it.

Abraham Lincoln had ideas that made him unpopular with his own political party, but he had an earnestness that enabled him to outride opposition, to outdebate the educated orators of his time, to hold the country together through one of its greatest and longest crises. Without earnestness, would he have been more than an Illinois country lawyer?

Without earnestness would he have been able to lead himself?

He failed in business as a young man, but worked seventeen years to pay off the debts.

When he first ran for Congress he was beaten.

Then he was turned down when he tried to get a job in the land office.

Next he was snowed under when he ran for the Senate.

Then he lost the nomination for Vice-president.

And was again beaten when he ran for the Senate.

But he was not defeated as long as he kept his earnestness.

He was no smoothie, just an "Illinois Ape," his enemies said. But with earnestness in abundance, appearance does not count.

Remember the story of Lincoln when you need to give yourself another injection of earnestness.

The leader has to overcome opposition continually.

FOREMEN BELIEVED TO BE SINCERE
GOT BETTER RESULTS

Degree of satisfaction
with conferences:

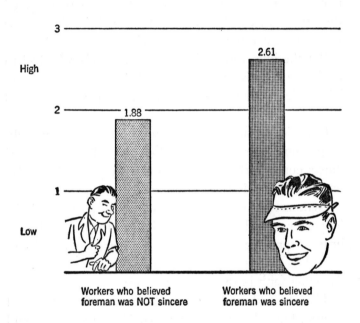

Workers who believed   Workers who believed
foreman was NOT sincere   foreman was sincere

Telephone linemen and installers were dissatisfied with the
system used by foremen in rating the quality of their work.
The foremen of 12 crews sat down to talk it over with them,
iron out the difficulties, and let the men know they were fair
in rating them. These conferences produced least change in
attitudes in those crewmen who thought the meetings were
unsatisfactory and that the boss was insincere. Data reported
by Dr. Alvin Zander and John Gyr of the Research Center
for Group Dynamics at the University of Michigan.

79

There is nothing like earnestness to win others to your side, to win a following.

One of my most promising students made the mistake of going into the wrong business. He had many offers in his senior year at college and took the one that offered the largest pay check. It was a patent-medicine firm whose products he considered a harmless joke.

But the joke was no longer harmless when he had to apologize for his firm or try to laugh away attacks on it by Federal and medical bodies. The big pay soon seemed sour.

His bride wanted him to stay with the company only long enough to save up a good nest egg. But unexpected illness cut into the nest egg, and a baby daughter, also unexpected, made it more difficult to save.

Gene stayed on longer than he wanted to, and the longer he stayed the less heart he had for his work. His brilliant promise was changed into mediocre performance. His faith in himself began to slump along with his declining faith in the business.

Then he had some good luck. He was fired. Stunned at first, Gene looked for counsel. He agreed he should be in something that he felt, from the bottom of his heart, to be worth while.

In his thrifty Scotch way he had always admired the work of savings and loan associations, so he went to work for one, at the bottom of the ladder and at a fraction of his previous salary. Five years later he was assistant manager of the association and one of the leaders in his small city. He had achieved earnestness.

Fate brought earnestness back to Seth.

Luck got it back for Gene.

Every leader gets it, somehow, somewhere.

Some leaders pretend to have it until they find the real article.

It was no pretense with Olaf. A Norwegian immigrant, he took a Y.M.C.A. night course in public speaking to help him learn English. At the close of the course six members were chosen for a public competition. Olaf was among the six, because the director wanted to demonstrate the progress that the foreign-born can make.

Olaf's English was still badly bent, but Olaf's earnestness was straight as an arrow.

He was to speak on the invasion of his native Norway, which had taken place only a few months before the contest, a topic that gave him added earnestness.

He started his talk in peculiar English, but with old-fashioned earnestness. He talked faster. He began to thresh his arms around. He could not think of English words fast enough to keep up with his mounting earnestness, so he lapsed into Norwegian without knowing it—and the audience scarcely noticed it, either.

Olaf was supposed to talk for five minutes. Though not a person understood a word he said after the first minute, the chairmen let Olaf go on for twelve minutes.

Olaf's speech, which no one understood, got the prize.

He held audience and judges in the palm of his hand by the power of earnestness.

Talk and act as if you meant it, not in a way to arouse antagonism, but with friendly, deadly earnestness.
There is real power in being sincere and showing it.

7 FRIENDLINESS
to overcome opposition

He was like King Midas. Everything he touched turned to money—except people.

Fortune had abetted every effort of this white-haired man. Born on a marginal farm, he could now look back over those hard early years as he sat on the gallery of his lakeside estate. His business, built by his own efforts, spread over several eastern states and gave a livelihood to more than a thousand employees—partners, as he wanted to call them.

He had recently arranged, in all sincerity, for the entire profits from his business to go to the workers. But their reception of this news astonished him.

"The old man is just trying to beat the taxes," some of them said.

"His conscience is troubling him," others said.

"Look what he's been holding out all these years," still others observed.

And, for the first time in the forty-year history of his business, his employees began to form a union.

"What makes people like that?" He appealed to me.

"Hostile, suspicious. You'd think they would show some appreciation!"

He had always expected a good day's work and had always paid well for it, but he had worked so hard himself that he had not taken time to show appreciation for little things, to be friendly. This crisis in his declining years brought home a great truth in human relations that he had neglected to practice. Good pay, even a share in all the profits, could not take the place of this missing element.

This element's power to overcome opposition in human relations was dramatically illustrated to me recently in Chicago. The dining room in one of the hotels looks out over Lake Michigan. The view is inspiring. Although the prices are more than I can afford, occasionally I pretend to be a corporation president and splurge by starting the day with this view across the lake while I breakfast.

An impatient businessman, in too much of a hurry to notice the view, was at a near-by table. He beckoned his waiter, a husky young fellow, to make some minor complaint. The young waiter stiffened in resentment. There was a slight snarl of disgust on his lip.

"It's too bad," the waiter said, "but there is nothing I can do about it."

The businessman automatically echoed the surly attitude. He called the head waiter and complained, not only about the food, but also about his waiter.

In great contrast was the old waiter who was serving two middle-aged ladies at the neighboring table. They were apparently trying to act like duchesses. They were being so particular about selecting their breakfast that I felt sorry for their waiter.

He was tiny and withered. His yellowish face suggested poor health. His smile revealed chalky white false teeth that bobbed loosely as he talked.

One of the ladies asked for pink grapefruit, which was not on the menu.

"Let me see if I can get it," the old man said as he started to hobble toward the kitchen.

In a few minutes he reappeared, smiling, but minus the pink grapefruit. When he reached their table, he bowed from the waist before the would-be duchesses, and said:

"The steward is so sorry, but this season of the year we cannot get good ones." He smiled wider and handed the lady an opened menu. "But perhaps madame would enjoy something else nice."

The old waiter was an artist in human relations. He had difficult customers to deal with, but he kept them on his side by using the vital element of friendliness. He undoubtedly knew before he started that long walk into the kitchen that there were no pink grapefruit to be had. But he did the friendly thing and won friendliness in return.

A few nights later I talked with several hundred industrial executives in Dayton. After the meeting a young engineering graduate, recently transferred from New England, came up to me.

"Since you have lived both in the Middle West and in New England," he said, "do you think my wife and I will find the folks in the Central States as friendly as those in the East?"

"Let me answer for the doctor," a ginger-headed superintendent interrupted. "Were the people friendly in the East? If they were, then just as likely they'll be nice to you here. East or west, north or south, if you're friendly and neighborly yourself, you can count on folks being the same to you."

Through my mind there flashed a picture of two distressed artists, Judith and Frank. They had used their savings to buy a year-round home in a quaint Gulf Coast town. They lived there for eighteen months, in growing loneliness, before a neighbor visited them. Frank said the threadbare native aristocrats did not like outsiders, and he would be hanged before he would go out of his way to change them.

But Al and Alicia, newcomers in a similar locality only thirty miles away, were sublimely happy among what they called "the friendliest folks."

The natives were alike in both localities, of course. Pathetic Judith and Frank, like the young waiter, were not showing friendliness and naturally had little shown them.

Perhaps the young waiter was friendly at heart but had the misfortune to have a customer who taxed human nature. And he thoughtlessly reflected back to the grumbling customer the same antagonistic attitude. People are like mirrors: Smile and the world smiles back, scowl and the whole world scowls.

The follower lets the attitudes of others determine his. He becomes a Little Sir Echo. The leader forces himself to assume a constructive attitude, regardless of what is being shown toward him.

We can do a black-out if we pretend not to notice their surly manners and assume a pleasant, friendly attitude of our own.

Keep your own manner and attitude friendly; the others will reflect it soon. Our King Midas had been too busy to think of this, but the leader should never be too busy to have a friendly attitude.

An old textile firm, with half a dozen plants in the North, began to start new factories in the South. One evening I asked Ralph, their general manager, what tangible advantages they found in the South.

"It is difficult to figure out on a ledger sheet," he told me. "But the day before we opened our first plant in Dixie something happened that influenced me to move other plants there as quickly as possible.

"I was in the local superintendent's office, ironing out some details. His secretary said a man from the state capitol was waiting to see us. We glanced at each other. 'Godfrey,' I said, 'they won't even let us get started before they begin making it tough for us. Oh, well. We might as well be decent to him, anyway.'

"So we went and greeted him. We offered to let one of our stenographers go through the plant with us to make note of the things he wanted done.

MORE FRIENDLINESS IN AND CONFIDING TO DEMOCRATIC LEADERS

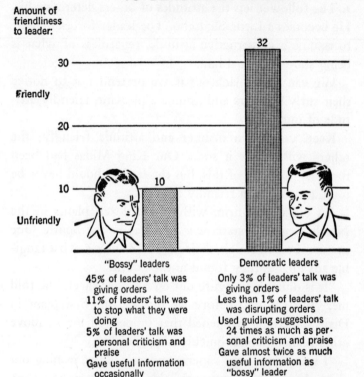

Amount of
friendliness
to leader:

30

Friendly

20

10

Unfriendly

32

10

"Bossy" leaders

45% of leaders' talk was
giving orders
11% of leaders' talk was
to stop what they were
doing
5% of leaders' talk was
personal criticism and
praise
Gave useful information
occasionally
Gave them little chance
to plan for selves
Almost no jovial behavior
or confiding with them

Democratic leaders

Only 3% of leaders' talk was
giving orders
Less than 1% of leaders' talk
was disrupting orders
Used guiding suggestions
24 times as much as per-
sonal criticism and praise
Gave almost twice as much
useful information as
"bossy" leader
Gave 13 times as many chances for self · direction
8 times as much friendly
give · and · take with them

Based on experiments with hobby clubs of 10-year-old boys
who worked together in groups of 5. The adult leader used
"bossy" style for 6 weeks with one group, then switched to
democratic style as he went to another group. Data reported
by Drs. Ralph White and Ronald Lippitt.

" 'Oh, no, sir,' the state man replied. 'I just came down as the governor's representative. He is very sorry that he could not come personally, but he wants me, sir, to tell you how welcome we want you to feel in our state.'

"It's that intangible friendliness, official as well as personal, that counted heavily in our decisions to open other plants in Dixie. I was all set to buck interference in the plant, but the state's initial friendliness took all the opposition out of me."

Start the friendliness yourself; don't wait for the other fellow.

As I sat in the back of a prosperous department store in western Ontario, talking with the seventy-year-old proprietor, a smidgen of a blonde, perhaps four years old, interrupted our conversation. She pushed a dollar bill into Fred Kingsmill's hand and said, "I want to buy something from you."

That was a broad order.

"I wonder who the child is and why she didn't go to one of the clerks instead of coming way back here to me," he thought. But he laid it to a child's whim and wrapped up one of the store's nicest handkerchiefs in a gift box.

He handed the attractive package to her, patted her head, and praised her pretty curls.

Then, from nowhere it seemed, a little old lady appeared. A lacy black hat and a black velvet ribbon accented her flushed face and twinkling eyes.

"Now, Fred Kingsmill," she said, tapping his arm with

her fan to emphasize the words, "you have sold things to five generations of my family."

She had made a two-hundred-mile trip to bring her great-granddaughter to buy something from one of the friendliest men in the Dominion. For it was friendliness that had expanded his business from a peddler's pack into the dominant store in the region. Friendliness spread through the organization and enabled another addition to be made to the store while cut-price chain stores were closing down.

This friendliness made Fred's capable department heads turn down flattering offers from the large Toronto stores. It was friendliness that mysteriously paid employees' hospital and nursing bills.

If the little girl with the blond curls had not shown me the secret of Fred's leadership, I would have learned it as we walked down to visit the large canteen he helped provide for service men. Every person we met spoke to him and smiled. People across the street waved or gave a nod of greeting to him and a smile.

The power of friendliness made Fred seem more like a young man of thirty than his threescore and ten. His friendliness did things to others, too. It drew people of all creeds and races together to cooperate enthusiastically in community betterment activities that Fred started. Professional men and down-and-outers worked side by side under the magic of Fred's smiling friendliness. Labor unions and capitalists were brought together for civic work by his friendliness.

Fred is one of the richest people I have ever met. True, he does not have a hoard of money to give away. He cannot pay handsome salaries. He does not entertain lavishly or bestow costly gifts.

But he overflows with the gold of sincere friendliness and gets in return a self-satisfaction, an influence, and a power with people that all the money in the mint could not buy.

He does not wait to see if people will like him. Fred assumes they do like him. That is one of his secrets.

He does not wait for them to say "Hello," or smile first. He takes the friendly lead himself, and everyone follows. That is another of the secrets.

He does not question whether or not he will like a person or wait before deciding to be friendly. He takes it for granted he will like everyone on first sight. This is the third secret of friendliness.

He magnifies others' good points, no matter how inconsequential. He overlooks the few annoying qualities or major bad points. This is a fourth element in contagious friendliness.

Friendliness is very contagious. The trouble is that many of us wait to catch it from someone else instead of giving the other fellow a chance to catch it from us.

I had to learn about the contagion of friendliness the hard way. When, as a young college professor, I was occasionally asked to give lectures to various groups, I took myself pretty seriously. During the introduction of "our speaker for today" I would scowl at the audience through my horn-rimmed glasses with what I thought was academic dignity. The dignified frown was mostly stage fright!

Without realizing it, I was daring them to be friendly. They always took the dare, and I always lost.

One evening in Cleveland a white-haired physicist, who bubbled with friendliness, said to me, "You do like people, don't you?"

Of course. Why did he wonder about it?

"Then let them know it when you are sitting on the platform," Dayton Miller told me. "Don't look at the audience as if it gave you a stomach-ache. Look at the folks as friends. Pick out one face and smile a little, then another. And when you get up to talk, talk to them as friends. You can completely change an audience just by letting them know you are friendly. They want to be friendly themselves, or they wouldn't be out to look at you, so give them something friendly to look at. I know you are friendly, but I would not have suspected it to-night."

At Youngstown the next evening there was the same sort of audience. But never before had I talked to such a friendly group. I knew that before I had said a word. They followed every word intently, although it was the same old talk that had apparently bored other audiences. They laughed with me at jokes previous audiences had missed. At the close they applauded so vigorously it nearly made me cry. For the first time, people came up afterward to ask a question or to thank me.

Yes. Friendliness *is* catching. An entire audience or a large organization can catch it.

A friendly manner gets attention and cooperation that are beyond purchase. Recently I was reminded of this as I rode through the winding valleys of Vermont on an otherwise dull train ride.

It was in one of those combination cars that had only one dining table. The sole attendant was cook, waiter, conductor, and bottle washer. It didn't give him much time to watch the beautiful New England hillsides.

One of the diners was a prosperous man of the world who was still grumbling about the customs inspectors. He ordered ham and eggs and gave detailed instructions for their cooking. The small dining facilities were a joke to him. He was annoyed with the many twists and bends in the tracks. He sent all his silver into the kitchen to be washed again. "In hot water, and with soap," he called after the man. I bet his wife was glad when business trips kept him away from home!

The ham and eggs were about half consumed when a timid, plainly dressed man took the fourth place at the table. His hands were calloused, his fingernails in slight mourning. His weatherbeaten face and rumpled suit were akin. He smiled to each of us as he inquired, hesitatingly, "I suppose it's all right for me to sit here?"

"That ham smells mighty good," he told the waiter. "And may I have eggs with it?"

He marveled at the compact arrangement of kitchen and dining quarters, said his wife had a kitchen as big as the whole car but couldn't make any better ham and eggs. He tried to talk about the scenery to the man of the world, but the latter was concealed in the financial pages and pretended not to hear.

When the man of the world left the table, he conspicuously plunked a half-dollar tip beside his plate. The waiter saw this generous tip but made no attempt to help the man as a jolt made him stumble over the chair when leaving the table.

The weatherbeaten man counted out the exact small change for his dinner. Then, glancing across at the half dollar, he took out an additional nickel and put it beside his plate. When he was about to leave, the waiter smilingly helped him with his chair and handed him the newspaper the other had left behind.

"If you get tired of watching the hills, sir," the waiter said, "you may enjoy reading the paper. I hope you have a pleasant journey."

The plain man just naturally used the four secrets of friendliness and got more for his nickel than the other got for a tip ten times that size. It does not take money to get friendliness, to dispel opposition.

Many industrial problems have been solved the friendly way. There is the Pennsylvania factory, for instance, where some 1,500 people make gears for army tanks. Several times the plant almost won an Army-Navy "E" for its part in the war effort.

The poor record of a single department cost them this prize. Too much absenteeism and too much labor bickering in this department cost the entire factory the award. An engineering-college graduate was in charge of the offending department. A slide rule was his boon companion and he tried to run everything, including the employees, by cold calculations.

The graduate engineer was shifted to the laboratory, and Al was put in charge of the bottleneck department.

Al had come up the hard way. At twelve he ran away from home because he thought his stepmother abused him. His education had been picked up on the run, at Y.M.C.A. night schools and from correspondence courses. Al had also learned much from the University of Daily Life, which had taught him the value of friendliness but not the perpetual use of a slide rule.

Al did not bawl a man out for being absent. He did not calculate on a slide rule the number of gears the day's loss put them behind quota. Al simply stopped by the worker's bench, smiled and said, "My, I'm glad to see you back. I missed you yesterday and was afraid maybe you were sick. I was going to go by your house tonight to see if I could do something for you."

Fewer and fewer days were lost from work. Bickerings over discrimination, favoritism, and rates dissolved.

Al was all business. He did not overlook things, but he looked at everyone in a friendly fashion. The men caught this friendliness.

Early in 1943, Al was just one of the spectators when the general from Washington presented the Army-Navy "E" to his plant. Many who knew the inside story, however, felt the pennant should have been handed first to

Al, then to the general manager. And that it should have been an "F" for the power of friendliness. For Al just naturally:

Assumed that people would like him.

Took the friendly lead.

Assumed he would like everyone—and did.

And kept his eyes on the good points of others.

8 GOOD-FINDING
to uncover ability

A leader is known by the men he develops. Andrew Carnegie, who started from scratch himself, developed forty-three millionaires who also started from scratch. The great industries he started are going strong today, since he developed men who could carry on, and they, in turn, carried on the practice of developing younger men.

This is one of the great advantages to industry in a democracy.

Stinnes expanded great factory systems in Germany, but, unlike Carnegie, he did not develop men to carry on. Two years after Stinnes's death his industries were disintegrating.

I was reminded of this at a man-power conference in the Second World War. A thoroughly patriotic general manager of a sizable Atlantic Coast factory complained about the difficulty of locating men who could share the responsibilities of running his greatly expanded facilities.

"I'm not surprised," my companion whispered to me. "The old so-and-so has done nothing to develop his own men so they could carry bigger jobs. Now he has to go out in the market and pay a fancy figure. We have had no shortage; we've been developing our junior men for years and they step right into bigger jobs and the whole shebang hums without a hitch."

A good many years ago the directors of a struggling but promising company looked around for a new president. The man of their choice was energetic Thomas J. Watson. They told him he'd probably have to look around outside and hire a group of men to help him run the business and get rid of the deadwood among the executives.

"If your business is as far gone as that," Watson informed them, "I will clear out of a hopeless situation, too. But you are all wrong. You have enough talent here to run a business many times as large, if you develop it. My pleasure will be, not to go out and search for world-beaters to come in and help me run the business, but to develop the talent that I know already exists in it."

And he found the talent in it. He developed the talent and the gigantic International Business Machines Corporation.

The leader has to look always to the future, to develop the best in the men around him.

The hidden ability can be uncovered and developed best by good-finding, which is the opposite of fault-finding.

You will find the key to good-finding and see its results in this story, for it shows why some people seem to have the knack of bringing out the abilities of others. It is an unpublished excerpt from the life story of a singer

whom you have often heard featured on the radio.
We shall call her Isabel. She made her debut in long
dark curls and a gossamer angel's dress. Everyone said the
little five-year-old had the sweetest voice and the most
assurance of any of the local artists in the church can-
tata. The bushy-haired choir director, who flirted out-
rageously, told her parents that someday Isabel would
be a great singer.

At the state university, where she was in one of my
classes, the pudgy director of the school of music had
the same enthusiasm for Isabel's thrilling voice. She
played and sang leading parts in campus musical pro-
ductions with all the aplomb of a veteran star.

She went to Chicago after graduation, where she sang
in church choirs and at minor engagements while she
took advanced courses in music. One of her instructors
was a bushy-haired man who reminded her of the choir
leader back home. She thought old Fritz was simply wonderful.

One afternoon, during rest period, while Fritz was
telling about his childhood struggles in Vienna, Isabel
realized she was in love. In a few months she was married to this man who was old enough to be her father.

They adored each other, and friends forgot the chasm
between their ages. Whenever Isabel sang, Fritz sat
where he could direct her, unseen by the audience. On
the way home he would point out her mistakes. He
wanted to help her become a great singer.

In their studio apartment he set alarm clocks to time
her practice. He was always at the keyboard of their

old grand piano or leaning on its scratched top while she practiced. His trained ear caught the slightest imperfection, and he had her go over passages again and again until they were flawless.

They say practice makes perfect, but not for Isabel. Church music directors began to drop her as soloist, giving vague excuses. Her musical friends wondered, over their wine glasses, about the strident, forced quality that was appearing in her voice. Some thought her vocal cords were too tight; others said it was a nasal quality.

They were wrong. Isabel's spirit was breaking. She had lost her assurance.

One rainy evening Fritz went to the bakery and was gone for hours. Isabel grew more anxious by the minute. It was nearly midnight when a policeman came to tell her about the automobile that disappeared into the gusts of rain after striking her husband.

Isabel's friends were extremely considerate and tried gently to have her return home. But Isabel stayed. She did not practice much, for she was haunted by a familiar voice pointing out her errors. Engagements to sing came rarely, but she cheerfully pared down living expenses.

At Christine's one evening she met jolly, plump Roger, a securities salesman. He knew little about music, but he liked Isabel's singing. He asked her to sing again and again. He had a banker engage her for a banquet. He asked his country club to have her sing at their annual dinner. And he asked her to marry him.

Roger also persuaded her to practice evenings, so he

could hear her. He would listen entranced, applaud lustily, and shout, "Bravo! Bravo!" He would not have known if she had been off on a couple of notes, and jolly Roger probably would not have mentioned it if he had known.

Isabel no longer needed an alarm clock to keep her at her vocal exercises. Her musical friends began to talk about the wonderful new quality in her voice. Musical directors began to engage her again. "Perhaps poor Fritz was a better coach than we suspected," they commented to each other.

Again they were wrong. Fritz was an unfortunate tutor. He broke Isabel's voice and spirit because he emphasized nothing but her mistakes.

Unmusical Roger was the tutor who really helped Isabel up the shaky ladder to renown. He was not a faultfinder. Roger found only the good in her voice. For him, Isabel sang to get good results, not to avoid faults.

Thousands have ceased to try to do their best because they have been reminded only of their worst.

This is true even in schoolwork. Elementary-school children were tested with arithmetic problems. Those who had only mistakes pointed out improved 20 per cent in a week.

The others, whose errors were overlooked and who were encouraged for the sums they had right, improved 70 per cent!

Abilities wither under faultfinding, blossom under encouragement.

GOOD-FINDING GOT MORE FAVORABLE
RESULTS THAN FAULT-FINDING

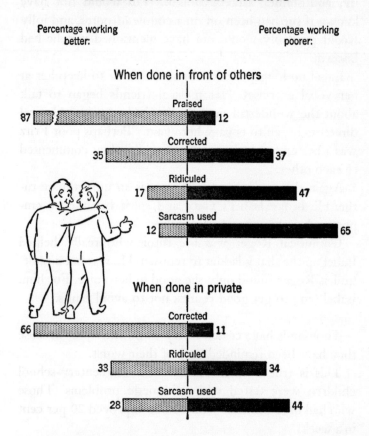

Percentage working
better:

Percentage working
poorer:

When done in front of others

Praised

87   12

Corrected

35   37

Ridiculed

17   47

Sarcasm used

12   65

When done in private

Corrected

66   11

Ridiculed

33   34

Sarcasm used

28   44

Good-finding in front of others was reported as almost invariably causing the person who was given a pat on the back
to work harder. Notice that there is least sting when the
faultfinding that has to be done is done in private. Data com-
bined from independent surveys made by Drs. Thomas H.
Briggs and Donald A. Laird.

102

I neglected to apply this basic truth a while ago when trying to teach tricks to our brown-and-white terrier. When Gypsy didn't perform as we wanted, she was scolded. She then flopped over on her back in submission or looked at us sorrowfully. I had almost given up hope of ever teaching her tricks, and had about concluded she was particularly dumb.

"The dog is all right," Perc said one evening. "You gotta know more than the dog to train one!"

I tried to laugh it off but thought of Fritz and Roger. I encouraged Gypsy when she started right and ignored her false starts. For two weeks I had been trying to get her to jump over my outstretched leg but had only been breaking her spirit by faultfinding.

By encouraging her moves in the right direction, in less than fifteen minutes she was excitedly jumping over my leg like the star performer of the dog-and-pony circus. And a few minutes later Gypsy came up and waited in position for me to put out my leg so she could jump over it again.

Then she perked her head at me, wiggled her tail, and I imagined she whispered: "See, I wasn't dumb at all. All I needed was good-finding, not faultfinding."

Early in the war a radio-instrument firm opened branch plants. Experienced factory men had to train new hands for delicate work. At the Pennsylvania branch the new workers quickly caught on and were soon in actual production.

But the New Jersey plant training did not seem to

bring results. The home office wondered if the Jersey employees were lacking in intelligence, but employment tests showed no difference between the two plants.

Investigation, however, showed that at the Jersey plant the girls were being told how not to do it. The instructors were looking for mistakes and stressing the difficulty of the work. The girls were on needles and pins. Many quit after a day or two because they felt the work was going to be too difficult for them.

At the Pennsylvania factory the new girls were being told, "You'll get on to it quickly. There really isn't much to it, but first we'll practice on some jobs that don't matter."

Faultfinding plants negative ideas.

Good-finding brings a positive attitude.

At an electric company dinner in Boston years ago a gangling engineer from a Detroit power plant sat beside a deaf man from New Jersey. The engineer explained some ideas he had for gasoline engines and different ways for transmitting their power to wheels on a highway.

Engineers and capitalists in Detroit found many faults with his ideas. The deaf man, listening with one hand cupped to his good ear, caught a tone of discouragement. He asked for more details. He nodded encouragement. The young man returned to Detroit, determined at last to see his idea through.

The world knows the results, but few know that good-finding at Boston that night by Thomas A. Edison kept young Henry Ford trying.

When you see an automobile, remember the part good-finding played in its early development.

When a subordinate comes to you with an idea, remember good-finding.

If the leader is a good-finder he can handle his employees so that their abilities are encouraged to develop.

Then, too, he will know better what his different employees can do. The faultfinding boss can tell what is wrong with each worker, but when emergencies arise it is vital for him to know what each one can do best. The habit of finding good gives him this knowledge.

For instance, at a foremen's weekly meeting some of the men brought up Old John for discussion. They said he was so vulgar in his speech that even a skunk would avoid him. Consensus of opinion, at first, seemed to favor a cleanup of the plant atmosphere by letting the old man go.

"What are his good points?" the superintendent asked.

He was the best diesinker in the state!

Then the superintendent reminded them of the time some moralists asked President Lincoln to fire General Grant because he drank whisky. "Find what brand of whisky he uses. Then get some for our losing generals," was his humorous answer.

"We hire men for what they can do, not for what's nice about them," the superintendent continued. "No one is perfect, but we have to keep looking for the few perfections people have and place them according to those, rather than ousting them because of some imperfections. Heaven help every man at this table if the brass hats kept a record of our faults rather than of the jobs we can turn out."

You can't build an organization on the basis of faults.

I wonder why so many successful selling organizations keep telling their salesmen time and time again never to find fault with competitive lines?

There are people who have the frightful habit of finding fault with themselves most of the time. They keep themselves at the bottom of the line.

Keep your eye on your own good points, as well as on the good points of others.

Late one evening I was the sole customer in a Greek restaurant in Charleston, W. Va. Two young waitresses were unburdening their feelings to each other, and I eavesdropped on their earnest conversations.

"So you came back here to work," the smaller said, "even though it meant less money? Well, I don't know as I blame you. Money isn't everything, and Mike sure is one swell boss."

"You bet money isn't everything," the tall girl said. "Mike here was the first boss I had when I came in from the farm. I didn't know much about serving food to city folks, and I guess I was nervous and clumsy. But Mike, he was so helpful. He didn't find fault. Just smiled and said I'd catch on soon and showed me how."

The tall girl brought my favorite piece of pie—apple —and returned to her conversation.

"Nobody scarcely ever tips here," she continued, "and they always did at the other place. But the tips didn't make up for the bawlings out. Honestly, some nights I was so upset I couldn't go to sleep and was all tired out the next day. After all, Mike pays as well as he can, and he is so considerate. So I'm back for keeps now, and really, Lottie, I feel like a dog for having quit. I was tickled pink when he said I could come back."

Scotchman that I am, I left her a tip and dropped my change into the jar of Aid for Greek Refugees, as part payment for the story I overheard about a good-finder.

9 HARNESS CRITICISM
in a way to win appreciation

Only a fool criticizes people openly.

Only a fool neglects to criticize people who need it.

The leader wins appreciation and develops his people by never failing to criticize those who need it, but by *doing it in the right way*.

Some bosses know how much everyone resents open criticism and are so weak-livered that they neglect to criticize their workers. This is real neglect of duty to the firm and neglect of opportunity to help the workers improve.

Other bosses like nothing better than to skin their workers alive with the sharp edge of criticism.

The person who criticizes when it is needed, and *in the right way*, is a rare specimen. He is the real leader.

"The trouble with the men is that they're interested only in the money they get," the production superintendent told me. "They've no more interest in workmanship or output than Paddy's mule. Blazes! We have to keep driving them until I'm sick and tired of it. And we are in war production; you'd think that would make some difference with them."

Half an hour later I stopped in at the lunch wagon a block down the street. I knew some of the men from the first shift would be stopping in for a cup of coffee on their way home. I wanted to listen to their talk while they were relaxing at the end of the day's work.

"Bad News Charlie was in our department, raisin' hell, this morning"—the young man with the missing finger started the conversation. "Saw him giving it to the foreman, so I ducked into the washroom for fifteen minutes to let it blow over."

The old-timer with the walrus mustache took a quick sip of his hot, black coffee. "Don't let it get you down," he said. "By the time you have worked as long as I have you'll be used to it and pay no attention. You'll soon find out that you see the bosses only when something goes wrong. They seem to smell trouble a block away."

He dunked his doughnut, then continued. "You'll never know whether you've been doing a good job, but just let something go wrong, an' you'll know about it plenty soon—and plenty hard."

"Yah," said the Swedish chap as he put the sugar rations of the other two into his cup and stirred with the handle of the spoon. "The only way to find out how you stand is yust to up and ask for a raise. It helps if you get mad. That's what I done. Threw down my shop coat, started to pack up my tools, and yelled yust awful."

I couldn't help joining in their laughter. But it was serious, and true to life the world over. In their little gripe session they had diagnosed one of the great weaknesses in leadership.

The production superintendent was Bad News Charlie. He scarcely believed me when I told him later about the nickname the men had for him. Most bosses have nicknames—used only behind their backs—that reflect their bungling use of criticism. No wonder so many bosses think employees have no interest in the work!

My first boss had the nickname of "Dummy." We used it right to his face. I have had other bosses since, including university and corporation presidents, who deserved the same nickname but for a different reason. Dummy, you see, had been born deaf and dumb.

Dummy had the physique of a Greek god, hardened by long years of manual labor. He knew all about day labor and a lot about human nature, although it was some twenty years before I realized this.

It was the summer vacation after my second year of high school. When Dummy saw the soft, gangling kid report for work he might have justly said something about sending a boy to do a man's work. But Dummy couldn't talk (if only more bosses couldn't!), and even if he could, I doubt if he would have said that. His own affliction apparently gave him an understanding of people that many bosses lack.

Dummy quickly discovered that I knew nothing about using a pick and shovel, but he didn't "lay me out in lavender" for not knowing.

Instead, he grunted at me, pointed to a couple of tools,

and motioned for me to come with him. I didn't realize it at the time, but Dummy was taking me around the corner, out of sight of the rest of the gang, to give me a trimming down. Kidlike, I was elated because Dummy picked me out of the whole gang to work with him awhile.

When we were out of sight he felt my muscle. It was like sponge rubber, but Dummy grunted in pop-eyed amazement at my powerful biceps. Twenty years later I realized he had been soft-soaping me, but I still loved it even when I realized it was phony praise.

After I had shoveled a bit in the new location, Dummy stopped me. He touched my shoulders, then made faces to indicate pain. He didn't need to tell me I would have sore shoulders. They were aching already, but I was glad he understood that.

Then he went through a pantomime to tell me that it was the way I had been shoveling that was making the shoulders stiff. He showed me how to push the shovel with my thighs to save my back and shoulders. He handed the shovel back to me, and I did as he had demonstrated.

Dummy beamed when I did it right. He nodded his head up and down and grunted approvingly.

Then he felt my muscle again and made a grunting fuss over it. He let me feel his muscle—just like marble—and counted on his fingers to tell me that in about three weeks I'd have muscles as hard as his. The liar! I'd never have those hard muscles unless I became the petrified man. But I ate it up and worked so hard all day that I went to sleep sitting up at the supper table.

In the years since then I have had many bosses and needed criticism from each of them. They all gave it to me—don't worry—but none with Dummy's expert skill.

Always follow Dummy's expert steps:

1. Criticize in private, not in the presence of others.
2. Do it with a smile, in a friendly manner.
3. Give some praise first to take off the sting.
4. Approach through the person's self-interest, that it will make it easier for him, not make more money for the company.
5. Make it constructive: show *how;* don't merely find fault. If you don't know how, keep quiet.
6. And end up with another bit of praise and a pat on the back.

Follow those six essential steps and you can criticize right and left and be the best-appreciated boss in the country.

A flying officer of the R.A.F., who received his flight training in Canada, told me about his first solo flight.

His civilian instructor was an old-timer in aviation, a Scotch bush pilot from the north country. After their first two or three flights in the training biplane, it was time for the solo flight. It was a windy morning, with the wind at an angle to the runways.

"Well, kid," the bush pilot said, "I guess now you can do a good job of taking her up yourself." And he nonchalantly walked back to the hangar, leaving the student in a clammy sweat.

As the student started the ship down the runway he cut a saw-tooth course but finally got in the air. His hands were so wet from cold sweat he could scarcely hold the stick of the plane.

His troubles really started, however, when he tried to land the ship. On the first trial he lost his nerve and zoomed into the air again, wings dipping one way, then the other. He tried to land again. Again his nerve left him.

"I'll be washed out anyway," he thought, "so I might as well land any old way. I only hope I'm not killed."

So he landed. He hit the runway hard, and the ship bounced 15 feet into the air. When it came to a stop he was ready to be bounced from the air force.

As he climbed from the cockpit, the old bush pilot came running along beside the ship and breathlessly shouted:

"Good for you, kid. You made it—and it's all in one piece! You've got the makings of a pilot."

There were a hundred things wrong with that solo flight, but the wise old flyer gave only praise at first. That afternoon he flew into the country with the student and landed in a wheat stubble where—in private—some of the blunders of the solo performance were talked over.

Bushy knew that people dread to be criticized.

But criticism is essential, especially for the young or the inexperienced.

The dread is removed and the resentment changed into appreciation when the criticism is made in private, preceded by praise, in a friendly manner and voice, to show how the person himself will be helped, and with a sugar-coating of praise at the end.

Constructive criticism is like a layer cake; remember the frosting on top, the tasty filling between layers, and the sugar mixed throughout the batter.

What happens when a public official is criticized? He hits back, blow for blow.

But do you remember how Will Rogers used to skin 'em alive—and they loved it! How could he get by with it?

The answer is the way he did it, in friendly good humor and with a friendly smile.

One October evening an assistant foreman heard me tell how to use constructive criticism. The following April he told me this story of what it had done for him.

He had been slipping on his job and was due to be let out. Things were not going smoothly at home, and this was reflected in his work. His wife was going home to Mother. Why was a puzzle to him, for he didn't drink, tear around, or abuse her.

But that October meeting made him realize what was wrong. He had been criticizing bluntly, at home and on the job. He resolved to do something about it, to follow those essential steps when criticizing.

The following morning he applied the steps at breakfast and was rewarded by the best supper he had had in months. He followed the six steps at the shop and by the following April was acting plant safety director, a job that requires constructive criticism 95 per cent of the time.

His hardest task, however, was to make himself smile when he was criticizing or at any other time. When he got up in the morning he tried to smile, but as he looked in the bathroom mirror his smile looked as if he had a bellyache.

So he got back in bed, to try starting a smile all over again. While in bed he recalled Will Rogers. The thought of Rogers made him feel pleasant, and before he realized it he was smiling.

He got out of bed and rushed to the mirror. Yep! The smile was still there, a real, friendly smile. It became broader as he was entertained by the thought of a full-grown man going through such antics.

So now, when he has a job of criticizing to do, he first thinks of Will Rogers to get a friendly inner attitude that shows up in the smile, then he criticizes:

1. In private.
2. With a smile.
3. Giving praise first.
4. Appealing to self-interest.
5. In a constructive way.
6. And with a pat on the back at the end.

Early in the Second World War a small New England plant worked 24 hours a day on war orders. They used a motley assortment of reconditioned lathes, milling machines, and other equipment rebuilt for the emergency.

On the wall of the owner's small office there was a single decoration. It was a small glass case holding a red lollipop. The proprietor told me its story.

"That is what built this business," he said. "It kept me going when the going was tough."

Two toolmakers had worked side by side for years in a large factory. Their skill made them the aristocrats of the plant and was reflected in their home neighborhoods. That was back in 1929, just before the men turned forty years old.

When the depression hit, the firm kept them on month after month, although there was little work. The company did not want to lose the skills of these men. At last the time came when the firm no longer had the cash to keep blond Frank and dark George on the pay rolls.

The manager explained to each that they were not being fired, merely laid off until things picked up.

Frank went home. He dropped his hat on the kitchen floor, slumped into a hair. He ran nervous fingers through his tousled hair.

"Marjorie," he said to his wife, "I'm washed up."

"I know," she replied caustically. "You're past forty and too old."

His wife and children left him alone for several days. They kept to themselves. The children stopped playing with the neighborhood children.

But swarthy George did not go directly home. He had a delightful, carefree feeling. He stopped at a drugstore and bought a banana split for himself and a small box of candy for his family. Still he did not go home.

HOW MILD CRITICISM HARMED EASY HEADWORK

Seconds to do
one work unit:

Fifty men and women were timed while they translated short sentences into an easy code. From time to time they were given mildly critical remarks. These slight criticisms slowed everyone of them down, by 8% on the average. And after the critical comments they made 55% more errors. Data from experiments by Drs. Arthur W. Combs and Charles Taylor.

He walked several blocks to a hardware store and bought some tools.

When George entered his kitchen it was dusk. He greeted Peg, his wife, with the box of candy.

"What have you been up to?" she asked.

"Well, I won't be having much money for a while," he replied, "and I figured we might as well enjoy ourselves while we can." And he explained about being out of work, for just a while.

"Then you will have time, now, to put new cupboards in the kitchen," she said eagerly. "And maybe you can get some work to do in your shop in the garage. You're a fine mechanic, you know."

At suppertime his children were excited at the prospect of having their father home most of the time, as Peg explained it to them. After supper they ran to tell their playmates about the factory their father was going to have right in their garage.

Blond Frank spent most of the next day at home, listening to his wife complain about the world's lack of appreciation.

George spent it making a big sign that bore his name with the words "Machine Work" below it. He put this in the front yard, with an arrow pointing to the garage.

A week later Frank went to the state employment office but found openings for a janitor only. By this time George had his garage shop organized, although no customers.

Another week passed. Frank's wife was still grumbling, and Frank had given up hope of getting work. They were deciding to go on relief.

But each morning George shaved, put on his best suit, and then spent the day calling on garages and contractors to tell about difficult jobs he could do for them in his shop. He got no business. Funds were running low, and he pawned the watch his mother gave him on his twenty-first birthday.

Then one morning George did not shave, and his dark hairs made his face look smudgy. He was sitting in the kitchen, discouraged, when he heard steps in the driveway leading to the garage. He ran out, expecting to see a customer. It was just a little neighborhood girl.

"My mother, she says you can fix things. Can you?" she asked.

She was carrying a scooter, with one wheel missing.

George picked up the scooter and examined it. "Well, this is serious," he said. "But you came to exactly the right place. Come on."

He took her hand and led her into his idle shop. He spent an hour turning out a new wheel, while she sat on a bench, safely away from the machines, asking thousands of questions.

The new wheel installed, she scooted up and down the cement floor. "Gee," she said, "you *can* fix things, jim-dandy!"

Then she reached into her pocket. "I bought this with the penny I got for watching the baby," she said. "I was going to eat it myself, but you take it, mister."

She handed him the red lollipop and clattered away on the scooter.

George held the lollipop in his hand, gazing at it. Then he put it on the drill rack and watched the sunlight play on its shiny surface. It seemed to hypnotize him.

People will come to me, he thought to himself. *There is work for me to do. They do have faith in me.*

He slipped the lollipop into his pocket and rushed into the house. He shaved and grinned as he thought of his first customer. He put on his best suit, slipping the lollipop into the right pocket.

"So long, Pudding," he called to his wife. "I'm going out and get another customer. Don't wait the meal for me."

He visited the same garages again, keeping his right hand in his pocket. He talked with more assurance than on his former visits. Late in the afternoon he found the crew in a contractor's garage huddled around a dump truck. An important part of the dumping mechanism was broken. It would take a week or longer to get a new part.

"I can have a new part for you in the morning," George said. Then he squeezed the lollipop and added, "but I'll have to charge double time for nightwork."

The contractor liked his work and the prompt service, and soon George was busy. He added some machines, hired some old help from the closed factory. He tried to hire his old side-kick, Frank, but Frank was working for the government then, on W.P.A., and did not want to risk an uncertain job with his friend.

Before the war engulfed the world, George had a

dozen men working for him. Soon there were 130, most of them skilled toolmakers and machinists. Most of them, too, were more than forty years old, and so were most of the machines they used.

"That lollipop made this business," he concluded. "It showed me that others had faith in me. Peg, bless her heart, didn't criticize me for being out of a job, or too old, or not getting a customer. But I was beginning to criticize myself. And then along comes that youngster. She said I did a jim-dandy job, and she paid me in the most desirable thing she had, that candy.

"I keep it up there by the door so that whenever I go out into the shop, I gotta see it. You know what it tells me before I go into the shop? It tells me to talk with each of the men out there so that I help them keep their faith in themselves. The lollipop reminds me to sweeten them up."

I know of half a dozen executives who bought red lollipops to keep on their desks after hearing this story. The color is not important, but helping the other fellow keep faith in himself is important.

The most important job at times is to criticize, and there is no excuse for its being the job either neglected the most or done the worst.

Recently I was talking to a score of department heads of a large modern hospital. I asked to see the hands of those who, during the past 24 hours, had refrained from criticizing someone who really needed it.

Every person in the group held up a hand.

Then I asked how many found it harder to make the criticism after it had been put off.

Again, every person held up a hand.

Then I asked how many knew of someone, somewhere, who could criticize people so that it was appreciated.

Two hands went up.

Taking criticism may be more difficult than giving it. But many people have learned to take criticism without being upset by following these pointers given in Chapter 4 of our book *The Technique of Personal Analysis:*

First, repeat the criticism in your own words, and thank your critic for calling it to your attention. You don't need to agree with him, or to argue with him. Just repeat it back to him.

Second, ask your critic for specific suggestions that might help you. He may really be able to help you. Even if he isn't helpful, it will pay you to ask the question; be brief and listen while he talks.

Third, if some of his suggestions seem desirable after you think them over, you may want to follow them. No contradicting him; just say, "Let me think it over."

Your critic may not have been friendly at the start, but if you use those first two points you have good chances of making him feel friendlier. You will feel friendlier, too.

10 INCREASE OTHERS' SELF-ESTEEM
to boost loyalty

An unauthorized sit-down started in the crankcase department. The men were good and sore. It would have been laughable had it not been so human and had they not been holding up war production.

They were boiling with indignation because their supervisor had taken credit for an improvement that was suggested by one of the men. The man himself had not been angry at first; he just felt slighted.

But for several days his fellow workers had sputtered to each other about the unfairness. In a few days they reached the silly stage where people will bite off their noses to spite their faces.

In this competitive world folks often tend to help themselves out in competition by doing many little things to show off to advantage. Anything that undermines their self-esteem, no matter how slight, causes resentment, hatred, bitterness. It caused the sit-down in the crankcase department and causes friction day after day across the country.

Those who have real personal leadership control their inclinations to show up others. They go to the other and desirable extreme of building up the self-esteem of others. They laugh at jokes they have previously heard, they listen to a suggestion although they have previously thought of it themselves, they don't say, "I knew that before."

Pat knew how to increase the self-esteem of others. He was a trouble-shooting supervisor, a one-man flying squadron who gave hypodermics to departments where production was sick. Freckle-faced Pat was not an efficiency expert, just a whiz of a leader. He did not change methods or layouts, nor drive for harder work. Pat's secret was simple and one of the most effective in the world—he built up the men.

"I don't know much about this machine you are using," he would say to an operator. "You know it from inside out. Tell me what the tricks are in running it." Simple and sincere, yet it got cooperation and production.

The regular foreman had said, "I could get 20 per cent more production out of that machine." By thus belittling the worker, he got less production and 100 per cent resentment.

But Pat built up the operator, and he could count on loyalty and production thereafter.

The regular foreman had called his assistant a glorified office boy. Pat called him the brains of the department.

Resentment at the boss for belittling the worker is usually kept under cover for a while. But eventually the worker takes various and devious ways to even up the score.

Here are some things workers have told me, in their own words:

"I boiled when the boss said he didn't know whether a kid could do the job or not."

"After handling an assignment successfully in my own way for some time, the boss told me he would have done it much better in another way."

"I tried to tell the boss an idea I had for shortening our processes. When I had finished, he said he had figured that out some time before and walked away."

"The boss asked me to lay out a shipping container. When I showed it to him he said I didn't know anything about a carton. Then he proceeded to lay out one of his own. It ended up just like mine, but he wouldn't admit it. I lost respect for him then and there."

"The chief turned down a suggestion I made about a change in a job. About three months later my way was adopted, but he took the credit. Believe me, I've spiked him plenty for this since."

"I put the Red Cross drive on in our department, and we topped the plant. The boss took all the credit."

"The foreman messed up a job when making a change-over and told me to tell the department head that *I* could not get it running. I told the head the true facts in the case."

"I wrote a report for the boss but had to change the conclusions the way he wanted them. When the committee criticized it, he threw the blame on me. I'm going to get his job if it is the last thing I do."

These are but a few everyday industrial examples of

belittling the workers. It ranges from a condescending, know-it-all attitude to unscrupulously taking credit for oneself when things go well and blaming others when they go badly.

When the National Safety Council award was made to the United Air Lines, the company's president did not take the credit. "Air safety is teamwork," he said. As representatives of those on the team, he had a pilot, a mechanic, and a stewardess receive the award. No belittling there; instead, the self-esteem of every United Air Lines employee was raised a few notches.

It's a good thing democracies make it possible for people who are born on the wrong side of the tracks to become leaders. It gives us better leaders. I was reminded of this recently when I got acquainted with Elmer.

"Elmer has certainly made the plant hum, and this is only his first year," my companion said. "It's a strange thing, but our other leading industry got a new general manager about the same time. But what a difference between the two. Elmer is popular, his firm is booming, and there are no labor troubles. But the other plant— golly!—what a mess has been stirred up. You've seen in the papers about their trouble, and only last week somebody took pot shots at some of his strikebreakers. Pretty bad!"

"What accounts for the difference between the two?" I asked.

He smiled. "Don't laugh at this, but Elmer wears a blue shirt and drives a cheap car, drives it himself. He came up the hard way.

"The other fellow 'big-shots' it. He wears a starched collar, fancy tie, and a stickpin. He has a man drive his high-priced auto, like he was Morgan himself. Someone said at Chamber of Commerce conference recently that our town would be better off if this starched dude got down to business in a work shirt, like Elmer."

Even the taxi driver who took me to the plant knew all about Elmer. "As soon as I can make a deal on this old bus, I'm going to work for him myself," he told me. "I've always wanted to be my own boss, but they say Elmer is a swell gent to work for."

After all this build-up, it was a letdown when I met Elmer. He did not radiate magnetism. He was just an ordinary fellow, sincere, earnest, all business. He was cheerful and pleasant, but with no applesauce. He had a plain, rugged face, neither handsome nor homely. His hand was enormous, his handshake gentle. He was a plain talker with neither slang nor highfalutin words. His ready-made coat was hanging on the back of his chair. He did not look like a $25,000-a-year man, plus bonus on earnings.

That afternoon I watched some men bowling at the Y.M.C.A. Several second-shift men gathered there on their way to work.

"You should see Elmer bowl," one told me. "He never runs up much of a score, but he sends the ball down hell for leather. That's the way he does everything—puts all he's got into it and doesn't try to show up the other fellow."

"That's why he is a great boss to work *with*," a man from the adjoining alley broke in. The emphasis on the *with* was his; he wanted me to know he was not working for the company, but with Elmer.

At the dinner that evening there were some 300 of Elmer's top men. They had wanted to have an appreciation dinner, but Elmer would have none of that. A good, plain get-together, with some rare roast beef, was O.K., but there were to be no mushy speeches, just a practical, helpful talk on business and some companionship for an evening.

Elmer sat beside me. "What was the turning point in your life?" I asked him.

"Why, I've never thought of that before," he replied. "But there was one I cannot forget. My wife told me to pay no attention to my boss's orders. She, herself, refused point-blank to do what the boss wanted us to do.

"I was made assistant foreman in a hardware specialty plant in Michigan. The foreman instructed me to have the men call me 'Mister' and to move into a better neighborhood. My wife was delighted at the promotion, laughed at the idea of having the men say 'Mister,' and downright mad at the order to move into a better place.

"The only thing she has ever nagged about was 'Mister.' Whenever she thought I was feeling too important, she'd bring me down to earth by calling me 'Mister.' "

One time I had the unenviable opportunity of watching a big business in the process of decay. Such decay usually starts at the top and works downward. In this case the decay started with a former policeman who made stock-market killings in the middle 1920's. He bought a partnership in an important business.

Tim tried to conceal the fact that he had been born on the other side of the tracks. He wanted to forget his flatfoot years as a cop and tried to pretend he had been born with a brass hat. The company's press agent had to spend much of his energy getting Mr. Tim's family into the society pages. He had a phony genealogy cooked up. He could not resist telling people how much he had paid for things, and he was a sucker for paying too much.

One of the partners knew the organization could not hold up under such leadership and sold out. He is now one of their strongest competitors. Then another partner tried to oust Mr. Tim, but Tim bought him out and gave him a bonus of $100,000, with which this partner set up more competition.

Mr. Tim still has his coat of arms on his office wall and appears in the society columns, but all his paintings have been sold, at a loss, and his large estate is mortgaged to the hilt. Most of his key employees have left. He still can't figure out what is wrong with the business and thinks a reorganization would bring back the good old days.

The right organization would be a big boost, but Tim would never permit it. He would hate to see a chap like

Elmer, who does not belittle others in any way, sitting in his place.

Some time before the Second World War a group of German industrialists visited a business with which I was well acquainted. They wanted to see how it was possible for this firm to manufacture in the United States, pay freight to Germany, undersell them in their own city, and still make a good profit. Hoping to learn some trade secrets, they visited the competing factory in New York State.

The youngish general manager escorted them through the plant. He had been born on a sidehill farm, five miles from the smokestack. He had worked at the bench summers during his high-school days, as well as the next four summers, to pay his way through the lowest cost engineering school he could locate.

It was a hot, sultry day. He was in his shirt sleeves, collar open, lead pencil behind his ear. He looked cool. The visiting Germans were dressed for a directors' meeting of the gay nineties—striped trousers, Homburg hats, gray coats. One of them carried a gold-headed cane. Two wore pince-nez with wide black ribbons dangling from them. The fourth, who spoke the best English, was an engineer; he was the youngest of the visitors, and seemed to be the brains of the party of stuffed shirts.

The delegation created quite a stir in the plant. Old-timers still talk about this circus parade through the works. Pete, the general manager, in his shirt sleeves and friendly as always, led the parade.

The delegation did not discover any trade secrets. The secret that gave them tough competition was right in front of them the moment they met Pete, but they could not see it.

That evening, after a home-cooked dinner at Pete's house, the delegation was asked if there were any marked differences between the American and German plants. The man with the cane and the dueling scars, and the others with the beribboned glasses, were at a loss. They were thinking about the machines and processes, which were quite similar to those in their own plants.

But the young man in the business suit said, "In our country it would not be allowed for all the workers to say, 'Hello, Pete,' when they saw the manager."

That was the vital difference, but they did not get its importance.

Pete's attitude and entire manner helped each of the workers keep his self-esteem. He did not undermine their loyalty by belittling them in dress or speech.

It is easy to belittle the work done by people in the so-called menial jobs.

Before I was old enough to go to school I used to spend every possible moment admiring the man I thought was the most important person in the world. He was big, broad-chested, and walked with swaggering steps. In my eyes, no one could have been more important than he, as he dashed through our small Indiana town driving the team of Percherons that pulled our fire engine.

The firehouse was beside an undertaker's establishment that frightened me. But I would forget my terror of the caskets and watch Mr. Wilkerson by the hour as he polished brass or curried the horses as nonchalantly as he would have played with harmless kittens.

At school, in a few years, I came to the conclusion that the president of the United States had the most important job in the world.

Then, only recently, I learned about an unknown worker whose story revealed just what really is the most important job in this world. This is the story of a Welsh boy with the unusual name of Llewellyn Llewellyn Jones.

His brain tissues had been injured when he was born, and this injury kept him from having control of his muscles. He was a spastic, bright enough in learning, but unable to coordinate his movements. He moved in an uncertain and floppy fashion, made several starts before he ended where he started for. His intermittent movements made him the butt of boys' jokes and they called him Jerky.

Jerky watched while other boys played. He was not of much use at home, although he did deliver washing that his mother and sister did for the bachelor miners—his father had been suffocated in a cave-in.

As the other boys became strong enough—it was not a question of old enough—they left school and went to work in the colliery. They felt important then and swaggered as they told Jerky about their work 1,800 feet below the surface.

One day Jerky went to the mine.

"When I took Robert Roberts's washing to him last night," Jerky said to the boss, "he told me you needed a water boy. I could take the water around to them just the way I take their washing."

The next morning Jerky, as the new water boy, was loaded into a mine car and lowered into the shaft. He spilled much of the water as he jerked this way and that, but it did not matter for there were always a few inches of water on the mine floor anyway.

Many tunnels were no longer being worked, and he explored these, looking for short cuts. He soon knew how to get around to all three hundred miners more quickly than any other water boy.

"Jerky knows this mine just like a rat," one miner would say.

"Yes, a water rat," another would add, and everybody would laugh.

Ten years later Jerky was full grown and still water boy—the humblest job in the colliery, never before held by a grown man, but everybody understood.

Then one afternoon some frightened miners scampered to the surface. As they emerged from the shaft, breathless, the boss said: "Boys, I felt it in the floor of the shack. Where is it?"

"The props gave way in the Davids' working," they said, "and the whole north end is sagging. How can we get to the Davids boys now?"

"Come on," the boss said, "Jerky will know. He can lead us!"

And Jerky, the water rat, was the leader as the rescue

party crawled through a labyrinth of forgotten passage-ways. Booming, cracking noises echoed as they followed Jerky through the damp maze. In the excitement of leading the rescue, they said, his usual floppy jerking disappeared. He walked so straight that it seemed like a miracle. And never once did he let go of his bucket and battered dipper—badges of the lowest work in the mine.

After they got old man Davids and his three boys to the surface, someone missed Jerky. Several days later, when the ventilation had been restored, they located him, in one of the abandoned passages. The bucket was beside him, the battered dipper in his hand.

When the new water boy was hired he was given a bright new dipper. The battered dipper finally came into the possession of my English friend. He keeps it to remind himself that the importance of one's job does not depend upon the pay or the title, that every job is important if it is done well.

In the emergency, Jerky became the most important man in the mine.

One personnel man wanted to encourage the young people in his plant who imagined that their jobs were unimportant. He arranged exhibits to show the importance of each separate process and the way it fitted into the whole. This increased the workers' self-esteem.

It's how well the job is done that makes it important. Some apparent leaders do not have so important a job, on this basis, as the woman who scrubs their office floors spotless and shining.

Think just once before belittling an occupation.

In doing some research on General Francis Spinner, who got Abraham Lincoln to authorize the employment of women in government offices, I got acquainted with many colorful old characters in the Mohawk Valley. There was Terence.

Terence was proud to have been the third generation of his family to work on the Erie Canal. His grandfather had come from Ireland to help De Witt Clinton dig the canal. His father had been a lock tender and so was Terence until the canal was closed.

As I became acquainted with him I learned many inspiring tales about life along the old canal. His favorite story, for reasons I discovered later, was about the lad on the pig boat.

"Them pig boats had a horrible stench," Terence would say, giving a good imitation of the stench by a few quick puffs on his decayed pipe. "With a west wind, we could smell a pig boat afore she pulled into Rome.

"I noticed the lad that spring. He didn't belong on no pig boat—too decent-lookin'. He sort of acted like a whipped dog.

" 'Terry,' I says to myself, 'that boy has run away from his folks.'

"Well, I let their boat through the locks several times that season. The lad was keepin' the boat in fine shape, anyway as fine as a pig boat with a no-good, whisky-soaked cap'n can be kept. He seemed to love the pull horses, too."

Here Terence always developed pipe trouble and had

to tinker with it. He did this just to let the story sink in.

"Well," he would resume, "the pig boat hove in from the east late one afternoon, just afore winter freeze-up. It'd been a nasty, cold, rainy day, and the rain was changing to sleet. The Cap'n was staggerin' around the slippery deck, but I didn't see the lad who usually tossed the lines.

"When the boat was raised to the high side of the lock, the Cap'n beckoned to me.

" 'The young'un's in there,' he said. 'I'll leave him here with you. He's no good to me now—slipped and busted his laig a few miles back.'

"I went in to see the lad. He was pretty white, but there was no blubberin'.

" 'So you stove in one of your timbers,' I says to him. 'Lucky it happened here. Old man Sweet is one of the best natural bonesetters in the country, and we'll get him fust thing in the mornin'. Ellen'll take good care of you. It'll sort of take her mind off'n losin' our fustborn this spring.'

"All the time I was quietly figuring the Cap'n was glad to drop the lad off, to get outen payin' what he owed him. So I asked the lad how much pay he had comin'.

" 'I'll send it to him after I get some money at Lyons,' the skinflint Cap'n said.

"But I knowed he was a dead beat and I says, 'No, sir, you pay the lad now or leave one of your horses.'

"He grumbled, but I stood three inches taller than him, so he reached into his boot and paid the boy. That

RULES FOR EXECUTIVES

Aldens, Inc., of Chicago, gives its executives some copyrighted rules which were developed by Jack C. Staehle, director of industrial relations. Some of these which have significance for this chapter are given here, with permission.

He's important, too

Remember that the desire for importance motivates nearly everything we do. Make the other fellow feel important. Respect his traits and his troubles; recognize his birthdays and anniversaries, the glad and sad times in his life. Make him feel that he means something to you.

Know them by name

Speak to employees and acquaintances as often as possible, and call them by name. A man's name is the sweetest music he can hear. Don't wait for the other fellow to say hello, and don't neglect to say hello to the porter, the elevator man, the messenger. All of them have the same human traits as you do. All of them long for recognition.

Appreciate

Don't hesitate to give credit, appreciation and encouragement. If someone deserves a compliment, don't be afraid to give it to him. Go out of your way to do so, at least twice every day.

Listen

Be an honestly interested listener. Let the other fellow talk. Find out about his children, his mortgage, his ulcers. Find out what makes him tick. As he talks and you listen, he'll hand you the key to his personality. More, you learn something from everyone to whom you listen.

137

was the last I seen of the old buckaroo. I heard the next spring that he got done in in a fight in Buffalo.

"Well, mister, that boy worked wonders for Ellen. She had been pinin' after our own boy that hadn't lived out his first year. Doc Sweet got his leg set fine and Ellen took care of the boy like he was her own. He stayed on with us all winter, gettin' down a pile of wood big enough to last us a couple of years.

"He was a good churchgoin' lad. He got so he didn't look so worried, but I didn't ask any questions of him."

Again Terence would putter with his pipe. That was my signal to ask, "Didn't you ever find out about him?"

"Don't rush me now. It was when we was eatin' our dinner in the clearing one noon. He was stretched on a log beside the fire. He was quiet and dreamy-lookin'.

" 'You're pretty good with an ax,' I said to him. 'You must've used one quite a bit at home.'

" 'I grew up with an ax in Vermont,' he said, afore he thought. 'My old man is the best axman around Poultney. He always said I wasn't much good with an ax, not strong or sure enough like he was.'

"That whipped-dog look came back on his face, but I saw he wanted to talk at last. Just as I knowed all the time, he had run away. And do you know what for? 'Cause his old man could do things better than the boy, and he rubbed it into the lad! Yes, sir, the boy lost faith in himself because the old man took all the glory and made fun of the lad.

"You know, I think it's a venial sin a lot of us commit, tryin' to outshine the other fellow. I decided then and there the lad was goin' to outshine me in 'bout everything. At night I'd say to Ellen, 'Can't tell if it's the rheumatics again, or just that Nathan'—that was his real name—'makes me work too hard tryin' to keep up with him.' Then we'd all laugh."

"It certainly does take the starch out of people when others deflate their ego," I'd say. "But what finally happened to Nathan?"

Terence would reply, letting me outshine him: "I don't know them Latin words, but Nathan, he finally wrote his mother and when spring come he took the first barge through to Troy to visit her. He used to write us and when he got married he visited us on his wedding trip.

"We had a nice visit with him then, an' I told him he'd be happiest with his wife if he let her outshine him. An' he looked at me, concernedlike, an' said, 'Terry, you old rascal, is that what you discovered when we were around that fire in the woods?'

" 'No, Nate,' I says, 'I found that out from lots of other folks. Everyone who's unhappy or discouraged has been whittled down by someone. An' folks is whittled down mighty easy. Watch it with that colleen bawn of yours.'

"Some years later, Nate owned a big sawmill, I guess the biggest in Vermont. He came down one day in an automobile, the first around here. He took us up to Vermont for a visit with him. Ellen was so nervous about ridin' in it that she went to church first.

"Soon after I got crippled Nate heard about it and dropped in one day for a visit. Mighty fine man he is— wouldn't whittle nobody down."

Terence's eyes always dimmed at this point, and he pretended to have pipe trouble. I knew why he had to choke back the tears. Nate had been sending Terence a comfortable pension for years.

Good old Terence—may his soul rest in peace—was laid to rest just before his eighty-fifth birthday, beside Ellen and his firstborn. Nathan saw that there was an elegant bronze casket and memorial masses. Terence was the last of his earthly line, but he left behind his philosophy of building folks up instead of whittling them down.

Recently a group of us were sitting around a hearth, watching the glowing embers. An aviation engineer was correcting and amplifying an incident his nervous wife was telling.

"That is the general idea," he said, "but you missed the most important details. It was like this . . ."

Whittling!

Later I told about Terence, and the engineer said, "The shanty Irishman was right, and I have always let my wife outshine me, haven't I, dear?"

How often we are whittlers without realizing it!

A college senior who was an amateur golf star had his pick of sales jobs. He had many natural attributes for sales success, and the firm thought his golf fame would add to his value.

However, he made the serious mistake of playing golf with his customers and, of course, played circles around them. The customers admired his skill, but were always whittled down because the salesman excelled them.

The firm's worst golfer was their best salesman. The customers would trim him without trying, feel set up, and buy to keep him from feeling badly.

I told about this, and about Terence, to a group of sales managers one evening. Afterward, one of them said that his firm had given up hiring men who stood at the top of their classes or had a lot of education. They were too apt to outshine the customers without realizing it. They had one chap—for a while—who even corrected his customers' English.

Another sales manager told about the great record of one of their salesmen who stammered. The man took a couple of months off to attend a clinic to cure his defect. His speech was improved, but his sales went down because he now outshone many of his customers in talking.

A retired Quaker schoolmaster in Philadelphia told me of his father's working philosophy for cultivating people and winning their loyalty: "Always leave others thinking well of themselves."

It was a cotton planter in the rich Mississippi delta who told me of a useful antidote when others try to whittle us down—and someone always seems to be trying to.

"I just think," he drawled in his rich, soft voice, "that folks who whittle at me are only trying to reduce me to their own true size."

Remember, whittlers are likely to let the knife slip and cut themselves.

Always help people increase their self-esteem.

11 JINGLE PRAISE
to secure best efforts

My grandfather was a smart trader. As a small boy I was always fascinated by his deep pocketful of silver dollars. I used to wait for those times when he jingled the coins. That usually happened when he made a farmer an offer for livestock. If the farmer seemed to hesitate, grandfather would jingle those coins gently in his pocket, and the jingle of good money seemed to have a magical effect on the farmers.

There is another jingle that sounds even prettier to human ears. It is the jingle of praise. Grandfather knew how to use that, too. So should everybody who has to deal with people.

It did wonders for a stage-struck cowboy. He was doing a rope act in vaudeville and finally landed on the program at the Amsterdam Roof Garden, which Ziegfeld ran for the after-theater crowds.

The cowboy sat alone in his small dressing room. His New York debut was a bust. He ran heavy fingers through his uncombed hair and stopped chewing his gum. His act was not going over. *Well*, he mused, *Zieg-*

feld will be sending you back to the cow country. He wiped beads of clammy perspiration from his brow.

"Hello, cowpuncher!" There was an angular-faced man in the doorway. "Mind if I stop in a while before the next show?"

It was the talent scout. *Going to let me down easy,* the cowboy thought, but he didn't know that the scout's job was to develop talent as well as uncover it.

The Westerner talked airily in an effort to conceal his anxiety. To his surprise, the scout did not complain about his act. Instead, he said it was one of the best rope acts he had ever seen. The cowboy was feeling better already.

"You almost make that snaky bit of rope talk," the scout said.

"Aw, shucks, I was just raised with a rope, that's all." In his astonishment at this praise, the cowhand fumbled for something to talk about. The morning paper was on his dressing table.

He pointed to the headline and made a pithy remark about it. The talent scout chuckled at the homey wisdom. The cowboy continued his remarks, making pungent comments about other happenings of the day.

Man! This is great, the talent scout thought. *Entertaining, and he is getting at the kernel of the situation better than most editorial writers. This is something new. Wonder how the roof-garden audience would like to hear it?*

"Listen," the scout said hurriedly, "can you talk like that while you work your rope?"

"Shucks, I've always amused myself thinkin' like that, and talkin' is about as easy as playin' with the rope."

"Good! Your act goes on in a few minutes. This time, talk all you can, just the way you have been talking to me. Talk about the news your audience has been reading, about everyday happenings. Take your time about it—they'll love it!"

"Aw, shucks, I ain't no orator, I . . ."

"Boy, you're a cowboy philosopher. Now go on up with your rope and *talk to them!*"

There was a fanfare by the orchestra, and the after-theater diners turned around. Just another cowboy act, so they resumed their chatter.

But, listen, this fellow is saying something. They listened and chuckled. They listened more and laughed out loud. Then they applauded some of his comments.

From a corner of the room the talent scout waved approving praise. To think that only two hours before Ziegfeld had told him to fire the rope act. Now it was the hit of the show! Those friendly words of praise to the distraught performer had uncovered a latent talent of which no one had dreamed.

A few words of praise turned the trick.

They were echoed in the chuckles of millions of people for years afterward. Remember Will Rogers, and pass the best ammunition for developing people, pass the praise along.

When Bette Davis made her debut on Broadway, her relatives flocked from far and wide for the momentous occasion. After the successful performance her father came beaming to the actress.

"I enjoyed the play tremendously," he said. He praised each performer, even the most obscure, but he never mentioned his daughter's success in her role. She waited for a word of approbation from him, but none came. That night she cried herself to sleep.

Some people are tight-lipped with their words of considerate praise because they feel that only the world's best deserve it. They neglect the opportunities that are always at hand. They praise the epic poem but overlook the thousands of little couplets. They praise the famous surgeon but overlook the woman who scrubbed the surgery floor spotless. They praise the fellow at the head of his class, neglecting the many accomplishments of the others.

Praise for little things counts as much in stimulating one to do one's happy best as does acclaim for the topmost accomplishments.

Forget looking for big things to praise; look for some little ones.

What should we praise people about? About anything we happen to notice. Has he tied his necktie with an especially smooth knot (it's a hard job)? Then tell him it's a good job. Do you think her eyes an unusual blue? Tell her, even if she's a perfect stranger, and she will walk on air for hours.

Does he keep his bench well organized? Tell him, although he may not be the best worker in the shop; giving him praise for a neat bench will help him become a better worker.

Is his handwriting particularly clear? Tell him, although his sales record may be poor.

Hard to find things to praise people about, you say? You're blind—or a conceited jackass! The next person you talk to, look for something you can praise—and praise it quickly and naturally. You'll be amazed at the results.

Praise counts most when it comes from the boss or from a close relative.

And, as the devil would make it, those are the very people who are most likely to neglect it.

The president of one of the country's largest advertising agencies has the devil's attitude about praise. Associates say he must have ice water in his veins. One of their biggest customers had written a glowing letter of appreciation for an unusual service. The personnel manager wanted to call this praise to the attention of the employees.

"No," the president said frankly. "The perfect doing of either the usual or the unusual should be taken for granted by our organization. We cannot tolerate less, and we should not praise them for what is normally expected."

It is easy to understand why he has to pay the highest salaries in the industry to keep employees and why his most ruthless competition comes from former employees who have set up business for themselves.

Often the praise that reshapes lives or gives the push for better achievement has to come—if at all—from a stranger.

One rainy evening I was in a restaurant in Chicago's Chinatown, dining with some people I wanted to impress favorably. We were scarcely seated when an unusually attractive, beautifully dressed woman of about thirty-five appeared at our table.

"Do you remember me, Dr. Laird?" she asked.

You could have bought me for a dime. In a strange place, with people I wanted to impress, and here I was approached by a vision in a Paris outfit who knew me. At first I thought I was the victim of a practical joke. Then I wondered if it were a blackmail scheme. I scarcely knew what to say, but that is seldom a handicap with women. If you just wait, they will do the talking. This woman did.

"Don't you remember?" she continued. "It was fourteen years ago."

That only made it worse for me, for I had been in Chicago all summer fourteen years previously, but I let her do the talking.

"You used to come out to the X Company." I felt better, for I had made several visits to that scientific supply house.

"I was Mr. Smith's secretary," she continued. "One day you had to wait while he was in the darkroom. While you were waiting you asked how I liked using the new noiseless typewriter, and then you asked if I was the person who was preparing the greatly improved mimeographed circulars the company used. I was."

Now she was sitting in a chair someone had provided. I was still too flabbergasted to think of that courtesy. She leaned toward me as she talked eagerly.

"That was my first job. I didn't want to be somebody's stenographer. I wanted to write advertising, but I had to take a job. Mr. Smith did not like the way I wrote those mimeographed circulars, and I was discouraged. But you came in—a total stranger—and praised them. It meant so much to me.

"That very evening I finally got up enough courage to talk the neighborhood restaurant into letting me do some direct-mail advertising for them in return for my meals. Later I talked the laundryman into the same arrangement. Your praise meant so much, you see.

"Soon I was able to devote all my time to my own little direct-mail advertising business. It grew, and I have partners now. We are all over at that table, celebrating a big contract we signed today in Milwaukee.

"When I saw you come in, I suddenly realized what had given me the first break."

I should have been elated to think that my casual conversation with a stranger fourteen years before had had such profound results. In fact, however, my evening was ruined. I even had no appetite for the Chinese food, about which I am usually enthusiastic.

How many times, many, many of them there had been, when, in casual contacts, I had said nothing to give people encouragement to do their best! Those were the things that kept passing in my mind and spoiled my appetite.

That chance meeting in Chinatown was more embarrassing than it seemed at first. It made me think of my shortcomings.

Remember the magic power of praise—praise for little things—even in your casual contacts with people you may never see again.

Don't imagine you are too big to notice—and praise—little things in little people.

Most people are uncertain of themselves. They treasure the reassurance that they are doing well.

I like to tell factory executives to give their workers a raise every week. When I say this they usually glance at each other as though I were a bit touched in the head. That is because they have their minds on the jingle of silver and are overlooking the best pay in the world, the jingle of praise.

They think a raise has a *dollar sign* in front of it, like this: $ raise.

The raise that counts more in making the worker certain of himself, that keeps him interested, has a letter *p* in front of it, like this: Praise.

Life should have been a bed of roses for Walter. He had more than enough money. He was deeply in love with his devoted wife. He had done Europe after being graduated from college with honors.

Now he was securely established in a job that he enjoyed and that would lead him places. His cordial hospitality and skill as an amateur musician made him popular, and so did his pleasing ways and comfortable good looks.

But Walter was unhappy. He had a dread of each coming day, of new acquaintances. He was never quite sure of himself; he always felt that he was doing the wrong thing or that other people were more capable.

Had he failed at something that would justify this gnawing feeling? No. Everything he had attempted had been singularly successful.

So goes the story with most people who are faint-hearted because they lack the steam to exert their best efforts. They can find no reason why they should lack confidence to go ahead, but there is a reason.

Walter's father was innocently responsible for Walter's faintheartedness. He was a brilliant surgeon. Born a poor farm boy, he had worked his way through college and to the top of his profession. Recognition, honors, money, all flowed in, but did not blind him. At heart he remained a frugal farm boy, striving to better his lot in life.

He wanted his children to amount to something. He did not want his wealth to make them soft or lazy. He tried to "stimulate" them to do their best by frank criticism.

For example, Walter came home from kindergarten one day with a drawing he had made of a cow. His mother praised it, and when his father came home, Walter

LETTING THEM KNOW HOW <u>WELL</u> THEY WERE DOING, HELPED MORALE

Per cent of men given pat on the back:

(Public utility crews)

High · morale crews — 47

Low · morale crews — 12

LETTING THEM KNOW HOW <u>POORLY</u> THEY WERE DOING, HARMED PRODUCTION

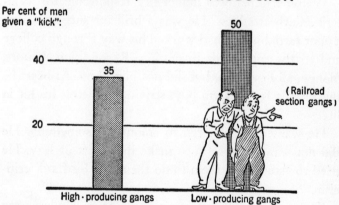

Per cent of men given a "kick":

(Railroad section gangs)

High · producing gangs — 35

Low · producing gangs — 50

Data from studies by the Survey Research Center of the University of Michigan.

152

eagerly led him to view this masterpiece of crayon art.

"Humph!" said his father. "Cows are not green. And this one has two legs too many; it looks more like a centipede."

Walter's childhood and youth were filled with similar opportunities for praise that his father didn't give, and this judging of childhood things by adult standards insidiously robbed Walter of his self-confidence.

Walter's father thought he was helping the boy. The honest comment was supposed to stimulate him to work for greater accomplishment. Instead, it made Walter feel incompetent, and he could not, as an adult, shake this feeling, especially since his employers and others never gave him a reassuring word of praise.

The best way to stimulate is to *say something encouraging or say nothing.*

Some years ago I visited a charming home where the mother knew the facts about praise and censure. There were four small children. The youngest was just learning to feed himself. Four spoonfuls would fall on his bib; the fifth would get into his mouth, at least most of it.

Ruth did not appear to notice the misses, but when the fifth hit its mark, she gave the little fellow warm praise for being such a big boy. He was judged by standards suitable for his age.

At noon the older boy brought home a report card that would have discouraged most mothers, but not wise

Ruth. She saw one "Excellent" (in health) and praised that to the skies.

The daughter rushed in, proud of an apron she had just finished in homemaking class. The seams were puckered and irregular, but the mother waxed enthusiastic about the bright colors and splendid design.

Eight years later Ruth was left a widow with scant financial resources. Then her rule of saying something encouraging, or nothing, saved her little family.

Stunned at first, the children soon began to work for the future with assurance, unhampered by the lurking dread of criticism or fear of failure. The older children got themselves through college, and the younger ones are on the way through.

And Ruth herself? She picked up her education where she had left off years before when she married and is now practicing medicine.

A courageous family, people say. Yes, the courage born of praise in the home.

The easy way is to censure, the strong way is to overlook . . . and praise.

Do you feel that public eating places normally give poor service? If so, you may have an attitude of criticizing rather than of praising. During the year I have to eat a good many meals away from home and I have discovered that I can have extra special service—even larger portions—by an attitude of praise.

For instance, I always manage to find something complimentary to say about the *first thing* I taste, and I ask the waiter, or waitress, to tell the chef how well I liked it. I don't wait until the meal is all over and then pass along the praise. Since I am a Scotchman, and a "good eater," I pass the praise right at the start. The rest of the meal is always served with a little more personal attention by both waiter and cook and the dishes are filled generously.

At a small hotel in Georgia, where I stayed several days, the widow who ran it said to me: "Have you mesmerized Beulah, our colored cook? This evening she prepared two special batches of hot biscuits just for you. If you stay here much longer, it will cost me money!"

I had not seen Beulah but I did know I was having marvelous meals. The only mesmerization I used was praise for the food and I always asked the waitress to tell the cook. It made Beulah forget the "miseries," pleased the proprietress, even though she pretended she was losing money, and expanded my waistline.

Try jingling praise about the cooking at your home, too. It will help your digestion.

If you don't use praise in handling people, you are not leading them. You may have methods for keeping them working hard, grudgingly, but you are not leading them.

If you don't praise those with whom you work, you are working twice as hard yourself and getting less co-operation and ability from them.

Even though you are using praise insincerely, you are still a better leader than you would be without it.

Praise does not need to be insincere, however. It does not need to be lavish, either; a touch of praise does a lot. Most people tell me they have to force themselves to start giving praise to others. They crave it but they are slow to bestow it. Once they start it, however, their use of it grows as they find the path smoothed by the real help it gives in human relations. Here are some reports, for instance, from one factory, as written by the men themselves:

"Operation 63 is monotonous. We had a large turn-over of employees, which cost us plenty. Our present crew has stayed longer than others since I have made it a practice to drop by each week and make a little favorable comment about something I see them doing."

"My stenographer is no longer behind in her work since I complimented her on some of it. I was going to ask for another girl for part time, but that is not needed now. Yesterday she took some spots off my hat with her type cleaner."

"I was surprised to find how praise works even on the low-level jobs. Lowest-rated job in my department is sorting scrap. I said to the scrap sorter, 'You've got sharp eyes for that sorting.' His work has improved since then."

"I got the service deliveryman to separate work on the last day of the week, a detail he usually forgot, by simply telling him that outside of that he was about the best deliveryman yet."

"An operator helped me on a difficult job some time ago. Later I told him how much it had helped. Recently he offered to do a similar job that he saw us starting, without being asked."

"The operator on a tough job was having a bad day with his setups. I stopped by and commented about how well it had been going with him before this trouble. It is the first time he has got through this difficulty without getting mad and spoiling a lot of material."

"I am fairly new here and was getting discouraged. After your conference my boss went out of his way to tell me how much two people with whom I had had dealings were impressed with the amount of information I had picked up in the short time I had been with the company. Although I knew what made him tell me this, it still meant a lot to me and helped me out of my discouragement."

"One of my men whistled most of the time, and it got on my nerves. I had been trying to screw up enough courage to call him down for this. After the conference I tried a different strategy. The next morning I told him he was the best whistler I had ever heard. That is all I said, but I am sure he doesn't whistle as much; maybe he was doing it just to try to get my goat."

What happens to people when they are given praise that they know full well they do not deserve? Listen to the story about an interesting old watch owned by a lovely Quaker lady near Philadelphia. It was a key-wound watch but had never been wound. Its hands pointed to twelve minutes past eight.

A few years after the War between the States, young

Stephen was jogging northward through the Pennsylvania mountains. He was on his way to his bride at a Friend's Mission among the Indians in New York State.

"See, Blackie," he said when he dismounted to give his horse a rest, "away through the haze in the gap, there is Maude, your new mistress."

Back in the saddle, Stephen talked to a crow flying overhead. He waved to a squirrel that was watching him. He tipped his black hat to a mountain oriole that whistled for him.

When they came to a roadside spring, he stopped and removed Blackie's saddle for a long noontime rest. He opened one of the saddlebags and, for the hundredth time, reread letters from Maude. He took out a stout leather pouch and patted it. The savings of his frugal years as a bookbinder were inside. With them he would start his own little business in Quaker Bridge.

As he was returning the wallet to the saddlebag, a crow's call startled him. Stephen hastily opened his waistcoat and stuck the savings securely next to his chest. Then he resaddled and was on his way. He wanted to reach Piney Forks before dark. A family of Friends lived there.

They were slowly climbing the valley east of Hick's Ford when he heard the caw of a crow. Looking toward it, he saw thunderheads on the western sky. Shadows of the clouds galloped down the mountainside and across the valley. He urged his horse ahead.

Soon everything was in shadow. There were a few drops of rain and the noisy cawing of disturbed crows as they fought for shelter.

Then the rain came in torrents. Stephen patted Blackie reassuringly and scanned the dim roadside for shelter. A gust of wind brought the odor of wood smoke. Ahead was a rough mountain cabin.

As Stephen dismounted, the horse whinnied. The cabin door opened.

"Hello, there!" a deep voice called. There was a huge man at the door, a rifle in his arms.

"We hoped to get to Piney Forks," Stephen explained, "but the storm caught us. Could we stay here tonight? I have the money to pay."

And he touched his waistcoat pocket to show where his money was.

"Well, that's different," the rough man said. "An' you must be one of them Quaker folks. Don't see many get-ups like yourn around here." And he laughed loudly.

They were almost through supper when there was a sound of crunching gravel outside. The pock-faced host went outside. Stephen could hear him whispering to a man.

"Somebody wanted to know the way," he said when he came back in.

Stephen and Mac sat in front of the fire. Stephen told of his plans—his waiting bride, his savings, how he planned to have his own business at last. In the flickering light he saw long scars on Mac's face.

Again there were footsteps outside. As Mac opened the door Stephen got a brief view of three women in a vagrant lightning flash. Mac shut the door and went out-side to talk to the women. Stephen thought it strange that Mac did not ask women in out of the storm. As he listened, he was startled to hear men's voices from these feminine visitors.

The Molly Maguires, that's who they were! The gang of mountain cutthroats who masqueraded as women.

Talkative fool! He was in the home of one of their leaders and had told him about his savings.

Stephen hastily surveyed the room for a place to hide his savings. Across his whirling mind there flashed stories of Indian massacres, in which the lives of Quakers had been miraculously spared. He relaxed. Stephen had reached a decision. He looked at his watch. It was twelve minutes past eight.

"More folks get lost up here," Mac said as he came in. He kicked the coals back into the fire with his rough boot. "Reckon it's gettin' bedtime."

"Yes," Stephen replied. "I want to get an early start in the morning."

Mac turned to him at this remark, with narrowed eyes.

"I wouldn't sleep well in a strange place, with all my money," Stephen continued. "I'm glad I found your cabin. You make me feel safe. I could tell you were an honest man the moment I saw you."

Mac kicked the coals, ill at ease.

"Please, Mac," Stephen went on as he passed the pouch of his savings to the cutthroat, "will you keep this for me? I *trust you.*"

Mac stood by the fire for a long time after Stephen went to bed. He had never been trusted before. Then he went outside.

"We'll have some sassafras tea soon. Remember you wanted to get agoin' early." Mac's ugly face was smiling down in the gray dawn.

"You're sure lucky you stayed here," Mac continued. "There's your pouch on the table."

As Stephen was strapping on the saddlebags, Mac said, "Here is something for your bride."

At Quaker Bridge, after the Meeting at which they were married, Maude unwrapped the small package. A Pittsburgh jeweler's name was on the box; inside was the key-wind gold watch.

They never wound the watch. Their youngest daughter, a lovely old lady of eighty who showed me the watch, often ponders over its strange message.

At First-day Meetings she is sometimes moved to hobble to her feet and retell the story. She always ends with the observation that "To bring out the best in people, we must let them know we expect good from them."

(Eleven Molly Maguires were hanged in 1877 for murder.)

The leader must be generous in his praise of others.
He gets credit by giving it to others.

Practice jingling praise in your own family. Make it a habit. Little compliments to husband or wife help human relations in the family. Children, too, can be handled better if they are given compliments for little things. Neighbors, too.

When you give some praise in the family—or to anyone—look the person in the eye when giving it. That is directness.

And don't pause after your praising comment. It will sink in anyway. It is more effective to continue talking for a moment after you dish out the good-finding.

After you have jingled more praise at home, you will find it easier to administer praise in the office or factory.

Have you ever realized that one of the best ways to get praise for ourselves is to give it to others first?

Chapters 13 and 14 of our book *Practical Sales Psychology* will give you many fine points on using flattery to build better human relations.

John Reason, Scotch factory engineer in Toledo, Ohio, wrote the following verse after reading the first printing of this book:

> He never spoke or knew our name
>   As he rushed by in search of fame.
> He had no rules as we could see
>   To care a bit for you or me.
>
> He always had a big complaint
>   When face to face with sinner or saint.
> He never cared how much we tried,
>   A chance for us was soon denied.
>
> He bargained for some expert who
>   Knew a darn sight less than me and you.

He spoiled our pride and then our work,
   From top mechanic to humble clerk.

His reward was loads and loads of trash,
   And when his bubble went to smash
He let out with a fiendish cry
   And blamed it all on you and I.

12 KNOW YOUR PEOPLE
to generate harmony

Old John started the factory, in central New York State, shortly before the Spanish-American War. He had been a blacksmith but made a few useful devices for the near-by farmers during the dull times between horseshoeing jobs.

Old John had good ideas, and his devices became popular. One farmer told another, and soon John had a business on his hands. He hired a few young fellows to help and then still more. Manufacturing was forced upon him.

His men worked long hours. The shop was hot in summer, cold in winter, dirty and smoky the year round. The pay was very small and the work was hard.

But the men liked to work for Old John—or, rather—to work with him. For John was right in the middle of things. He got as dirty and as tired as the rest of them. He did the same work and sat around the forge for half an hour at noon to eat a cold lunch from his tin box with the other workers.

They called each other by their first names and knew all about one another's families and hobbies. It was "one big family." Every man who worked with Old John would lick the daylights out of anyone who criticized the proprietor of the firm.

How changed the firm is today! In normal times they employ about six hundred men. The plant is well ventilated, uniformly heated. Some departments are completely air-conditioned. There is a clean, inexpensive cafeteria, a well-equipped recreation room. Pay is high, vacations are good, and the work is not hard. The employees today live better than Old John did.

Old John's only son—Young John—is responsible for these better conditions. Young John is a topnotch manager, a real businessman, while his father was a real mechanic.

The men see little of Young John, since he is in the office most of the time. The men work an eight-hour day; Young John works ten or twelve hours most days.

Everyone who is near Young John in the office thinks he is a great fellow, and the two men who do the hard work on his farm swear by him. They talk their troubles over with him, and he tells them some of his.

When Young John goes through the plant, however, the workmen make threatening gestures with rasps or wrenches behind his back, to the amusement of all.

Most of the men in the shop enjoy ugly rumors about Young John, stories about his daughter's operation, his redheaded stenographer.

Why do the men in the shop feel so cruelly toward him, while the men of a generation ago loved his father? The handful who know Young John and whom he knows stand up for him. The others seem to hate him.

It is because Young John does not know his people, and he is paying the price.

People crave to be noticed, to be known, especially by the boss.

They feel like fifth wheels, like worms, like Forgotten Men, when the boss does not know them. Yet as establishments grow it is impossible for the big boss to know everyone. The result is a constant struggle by sublieutenants to keep harmony in the organization.

In large firms it is an uphill struggle to keep a harmonious feeling, for nothing takes the place of being acquainted with the boss and knowing the boss is acquainted with you.

An electric-appliance manufacturing company, employing thousands of workers, once set up special facilities for experimenting with various working conditions. Their experiments went to pot, for they showed nothing about noise, ventilation, color, and the other things the firm wanted to study.

What happened was that as soon as a group of operators was separated from the rest in the small experimental rooms, their supervisors became well acquainted with them in a few days. Even when the experimental working conditions were obviously inefficient, the girls worked their heads off, for they were no longer working for a company or a boss, they were working for someone they knew.

An icebox company got a suggestion from that experience. They cautiously gave each of their foremen an assistant, to give the foremen more time to get acquainted with the workers. After one month they made this a permanent policy. The feeling within the shop, and production itself, had improved so much that the extra expense was more than justified.

It is a common observation that morale goes down when a shop is enlarged and workers doubled or tripled. This is to be expected, because the paper work also increases and the foremen and supervisors no longer have a chance to get acquainted with the workers.

Small departments have the best morale, for then the worker and bosses know each other better—it is just human nature.

And the boss must never forget that the morale of his people depends more upon how well he knows them than it does upon the money the company puts into improving working and recreational facilities.

Workers do not make menacing gestures with rasps and wrenches behind the back of a boss they know, unless the boss deserves the gesture.

Leonora has the most gorgeous naturally blond hair I have ever seen, yet, if I showed you her picture, you would call her homely, for cameras do lie.

The camera would show that one eye is noticeably smaller than the other and would not show the twinkle and the eagerness with which they watch a person who is talking. Leonora's eyes are pretty, not peculiar as the camera misrepresents them.

The picture would show a mouth with thick, protruding lips but would not reveal the perpetual smile that makes them seem pretty, nor the tinkle, like a distant sleigh-bell, when she laughs easily at your attempts at humor.

Leonora is really beautiful, when you know her, although her pictures look like a caricature. The tough breaks she has had in life have, fortunately, not kept her from acting beautiful. Her mother died while Leonora was a freshman in high school. Two years later her father was taken to the county hospital for lung diseases. Leonora was on her own.

She had real ability for artwork, but had to give up plans to study it in high school. She took typewriting and shorthand instead. After finishing high school she left her home town and went to Philadelphia. She worked in an office during the day and attended art classes at night.

She liked the office work, loved her art course, and hated the world more each day.

"Talk about the Lost Battalion," she told us later. "I was in one. I knew how the Forgotten Man felt.

"On the bus mornings I saw familiar faces, but no one said 'Hello' to me, no one knew who I was.

"In the office elevator there were more familiar faces, and once in a blue moon someone would say, 'Good morning.'

"And at the office my name was seldom used; nobody seemed to know me.

"I felt like a cog in a machine—just a number on the time clock.

HOW KNOWING THEIR PEOPLE
HELPED PRODUCTION

Per cent of supervisors
having high - production
sections:

Supervisors who
showed interest
in employees

Supervisors more interested
in routine than in knowing
their people

Work routine and equipment were the same in these sections
of a large insurance home office. But most of the supervisors
who were centered on their employees had high-output,
while very few supervisors centered mostly on job details
had high-output. One employee-centered supervisor said: "I
try to understand each girl. Knowing the girls helps with
handling the work here—you have to know what happens
outside, too, to help them in the office." Data from the Survey Research Center of the University of Michigan, Study
No. 6; survey supported by a grant from the Office of Naval
Research.

169

"At art classes, however, some of the instructors actually knew my name. One fatherly old teacher remembered some of my first efforts, and one evening he joked about them. I had actually been noticed! I nearly cried with joy. It made me feel like a new person—until next morning, when I was again unnoticed.

"How I longed for my Ohio town, where people knew me!

"Tell me, do you think I am abnormal or something?"

No, Leonora, perfectly natural. Everyone has a hidden hunger for attention, to be spoken to, to have his name used.

I spent a week end in a well-to-do home recently. The charming four-year-old daughter was so young and unsophisticated that she did not try to hide this hunger. She demanded attention, and I was glad to give it to her.

Her mother thought the child was being naughty and sent her upstairs—for getting the notice the mother herself wanted but wouldn't admit wanting.

I dislike to admit it but men seem to fail more often than women to give attention to others.

"Why take pains with my husband's meals," wives complain, "when he wolfs his food without even showing that he knows what he's eating!" Notice the things they make and don't hesitate to say they are good.

"I could go to a dance in my nightgown, and my husband would never notice the difference," another woman complained. Notice what they are wearing and tell them what you like about it.

At the shop or office notice little things about their clothes or their work—and mention what you notice.

Recently I was talking with some three hundred foremen in an airplane plant. They had not had much experience as bosses. I asked how many, during that day, had talked on business to a subordinate and did not know the name of the man to whom they were talking.

Ninety per cent of the men held up a hand. They had whistled to their employee or said "You there." They might as well have called the man a profane name!

These foremen had a difficult job getting to know their people, to be sure. Most of the workers were new, and each foreman had too many to supervise. That was not the foremen's fault, but it was their fault that they made no effort to learn the names of the new men. We got them to promise to learn the names of five of their men each day and to talk with these five men, calling them by their names, in a brief conversation about generalities.

Some of the men thus addressed went home afterward and told their wives what a swell boss they had, how wonderful the company was. Each man was a better worker, and harmony improved from this little thing. It is not so little, however, when we realize how deeply everyone craves to be noticed as an individual, especially by the boss.

Old John knew his men; Young John doesn't. The

bosses all down the line have to be as much of an Old John as they possibly can.

Old John knew more than the men's names:
He knew where they lived.
He knew whether they were married and about their children, if they had any.
He knew about their hobbies or recreations.
He knew their birthdays.
He knew their troubles.
Old John knew those things without trying. The community was small and the business tiny. Today the leader has to make some effort to learn those things, often in the first two-minute interview. He must talk with his people from time to time about those commonplace things that show that the boss knows them as individuals, not as production machines.

Old John knew his men without being "palsy-walsy." He was all business and ruthlessly underpaid his men for their long hours of work, but they thought he was a great boss because each remained an individual in the boss's eyes and conversation.

What do you think is the most vital statistical information the president of a company should look over the first thing in the morning?

The president of one of the most harmonious firms in the country came up through the ranks. He was with the firm from the time it was a two-by-four plant to its present big size.

He has one assistant who does nothing but keep him

informed about the vital statistics of the workers. The topmost report on his desk each morning tells about births, sickness, engagements, and other *vital personal* information about their force. He makes a phone call, drops a note, or stops to talk with the person concerned before the day is over.

He knows what the personal touch means between a leader and his people.

His firm's record also shows what it means to the people.

The old tailor who started what became a big business in Ohio knew that the rapid growth of his shop would leave many of the workers unnoticed and resentful people, so he made special efforts to know each worker personally, even when there were more than a thousand on the pay roll.

At the close of the day he stood at the door and said good night to each employee, mentioning his name. When he became too aged to do this himself, he saw to it that some senior officer of the company was always on hand to let his people know they were not forgotten men and women.

Do you wonder that, when the depression years of the thirties closed down similar shops, Mr. Richmond's was humming? The cutters, stitchers, everyone, hustled around evenings and sold the firm's clothing to their friends!

Would they have done that for a boss who was a stranger to them, who did not know them?

General Motors Corp. urges its executives to "Make the Howdy Rounds." While making the rounds they say "Hello," mention the employee's name, and spend a half minute with small talk that is unrelated to the job.

On these "Howdy Rounds," they talk about the other person's interests and hobbies and activities.

When a new employee is placed in your department, get acquainted with him as a person at the first break in work. Help him feel at home, and welcome. You can be aggressive about this.

But when you are placed in a new department, don't be aggressive. Keep your eyes—and ears—open and get acquainted slowly. But get acquainted so you know them and they know you.

You will find helps on getting acquainted as a new worker, or with new workers, on pages 372 and 404 of our book *Practical Business Psychology*.

13   *Leading—or driving?*

It was a foundry president who said farm boys made the best leaders. It does seem that in proportion to their opportunities, there has been an unusual percentage of farm boys who have made good as leaders.

The foundryman could not exactly explain his preference. He said that farm life made a boy more self-reliant and that the hard life of a farm made the boys more ambitious to better their lot. And, of course, farm boys are used to a long day of hard work.

There may be more behind it than that, however. Haven't you noticed that people who are good at handling animals are also good at handling people? Perhaps the fact that animals cannot talk helps. There was my Uncle Jack, for instance. He and my grandfather were stock drovers in the Middle West.

As I worked with them I learned a great deal about handling people, though I did not realize this until years later. I helped drive livestock to the railroad to be shipped to market or to pasturage to be fattened.

There were flocks of bleating sheep to herd along the dusty highway. Nervous and flighty creatures they were, so we took them along back roads to avoid traffic that would send them scurrying or into a huddle of fright. We would take them miles out of our way to avoid things that might upset them.

As a barefoot boy, I scouted ahead of the flock to make friends with dogs, which I kept entertained and out of sight until the sheep had passed. No nervous, jittery human was ever protected more carefully from unpleasant realities than those timid sheep. They were the prima donnas of the livestock world, the temperamental specialists, the flighty customers, the old-maid stockholders in prototype.

Sometimes there would be a drove of grunting pigs, as obstinate as a stubborn engineer. I still feel that the worst that can be said of a person is that he is pigheaded.

But I was taught to get them to go where we wanted them to by appealing to their natural weakness and thus not touching off their obstinacy. Their weakness was yellow corn. A small nubbin of corn tossed ahead of the drove, into the shade, was a hundred times better than trying to push or guide them.

I really didn't understand the dangers of pushing an obstinate pig until one turned on me when I gave him an impatient push. I quickly learned that stubbornness was not improved by pushing. Jack came to my rescue with a piece of corn.

The real fun for a small boy was driving a herd of steers. Any one of them could have trampled me without effort, yet they were tolerant of boyish noisiness. Had I yelled at the sheep, they would have frozen in a panic and lost pounds of weight. As for the hogs, a yell would send the ornery critters scattering in all directions. But the steers—I could shout to my heart's content at them.

Some would turn and look with a puzzled air and then go pretty much where they wanted to. We couldn't drive or coax the steers; they had too much life and might high-tail it over the landscape. We just sort of followed them along, easing a bit this way and that.

I thought of the steers later when I had a boss who thought the louder he shouted the better leader he was. He was a regular bull-of-the-woods, and how he enjoyed shouting at the hands. The hands were like the steers; they would have a puzzled expression of tolerance and keep right on as they had been doing.

It was at the stockyards near the freight station that I learned most about handling living things. It was an exciting place with a raucous blending of bleats, squeals, grunts, and lowing. It also reminded me of an oil refinery when the wind was right.

The animals were herded into small pens, like crowded refugees. The crowded conditions usually brought out the worst in their animal natures. There were fighting hogs to be separated, frightened sheep to be soothed, and sometimes a high-spirited steer to dislodge from the wooden fence.

Getting a load of stock to climb the narrow runway into the railroad car was always exciting and uncertain. They did not like to climb the incline—it was about like having to report to the boss's office. Some of the drovers used long pointed poles to prod the stock on their way up the incline. Others would get into the jammed runway themselves and kick and push with their high-heeled boots.

Jack could get a car loaded in jig time and with the least loss of animal weight. He had always had a way with animals, from his own thoroughbred horses to the mangy stray dogs he adopted. When he was loading a car he would get into the runway with the pigs and start scratching them. Pigs take to scratching just as humans take to flattery or a widow to lovemaking—you can't overdo it.

As Jack walked slowly up the incline, the pigs would follow along for more scratching. All the while Jack would be talking to them as if they were human friends. As the other porkers followed into the car, he would stand beside the door and scratch each as it filed past, just for good measure and to show no partiality—and also, I think, because he liked to scratch them.

Jack did not drive or prod them into the car. They followed him, and it takes real leadership to handle a critter as stubborn, or as dumb, as a pig, regardless of how many legs he has. Granddad always used to say that when Jack loaded a car they sent 2 per cent more weight to market.

My most unforgettable experience at the stockyards came one Saturday in the spring of 1907. Heavy rains made the mud almost knee-deep. A farmer, strong as an ox and locally famous for his Saturday-night drunken fights, brought in a load of hogs. They were fat ones, better for lard than for bacon. It had been a heavy pull over the soggy spring roads, and his horses were lathered with sweat when they pulled the load to the scales.

Uncle Jack looked at the horses, not at the scale beam. "Lew," he said, his steel-blue eyes narrowing, "you've been driving that team too hard, and they're one of the best pair of horses in the township."

I don't remember what Lew said, but I noticed Jack's words. He said them in the same tone he used when I tried to drive obstinate pigs instead of leading them.

After the load was weighed, Lew climbed back to the driver's seat and filled his mouth with scrap tobacco. He settled back in the seat, slapped the reins on the horses' backs, and said, "Giddap, you lazy varmints!"

The horses lunged into their frothy collars, much as the sheep jumped when I yelled at them. Jack came out of the scale house and stood with his hands on his hips, high leather boots ankle-deep in the mud.

The wagon started with a jerk that made the pigs slip and squeal in a tangled heap. As soon as the wagon was clear of the scales, it began to slow down and sink into the mud. The wagon stopped, mud halfway up to the hubs.

The horses lunged frantically, without teamwork, to budge the load. Lew yelled at them. Then he reached under the seat and brought out a heavy blacksnake whip such as some people use on tough-skinned mules.

He raised the whip over his head and struck one of the horses with a resounding crack. As he raised it over his head again, to strike the other horse, Jack jumped on the wagon and grabbed the whip. He threw it into the mud.

"Get off that seat," Jack ordered. "Those horses have enough to pull without your heavy carcass riding along!"

Lew sputtered something but remembered he had not yet been paid, so said nothing. But he was slow and deliberate about getting off the wagon. He wiped some tobacco juice from his mouth, with the back of his hand, and wiped his hand on his shirt.

Jack laid the reins loose on the seat. He stroked the quivering shoulders of each horse, patted their noses, and talked to them while he waited for me to bring some winter apples from the scale house.

The horses pricked up their ears when they saw him break an apple in half, expending in the exertion some of the wrath he felt toward their owner.

"Here, Lew," Jack said as he tossed an apple to him. "Frank Garvin brought these in this morning."

But Lew made no effort to catch it, and his apple disappeared into the mud behind him. He shifted his cud of tobacco and glared at Jack. Even a pig would have scampered for that apple.

Each horse eagerly ate its portion. The younger one, with a white star on its forehead, playfully nibbled at Jack's sleeve, asking for more. Jack gave him the rest of his own apple. By now the horses had stopped quivering.

Jack reached for the reins, patted the flank of each horse. "Well, boys," he said, "let's see what we can do."

He tightened the reins slightly, and the younger horse

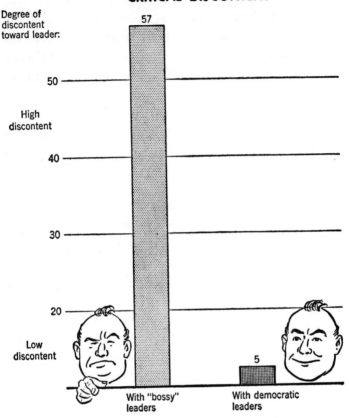

"BOSSY" LEADING AROUSED MORE CRITICAL DISCONTENT

Degree of discontent toward leader:

57

50

High discontent

40

30

20

Low discontent

5

With "bossy" leaders

With democratic leaders

The same boys, and the same leaders, are represented in both bars. The difference is due to the leaders' using "bossy" style part of the time, and democratic style part of the time. Fuller explanation with the cartoon on page 88. From experiments by Drs. Ralph White and Ronald Lippitt.

181

nodded its head and rubbed its nose against the other's cheek.

"Don," Jack said to me, "lay hold of the spokes on the other front wheel and help them out." He had the reins in one hand and was pulling on one front wheel himself.

"Giddap, boys!" he called to the team in a pleasant, firm voice.

That giddap did something to me, too. It was so friendly and reassuring. I tugged on the front wheel with all my boyish strength, and my red rubber boots sunk into the mud.

That giddap did something to the horses, too. It was the same voice that had just given them the apple and talked to them. They stretched into their collars and pulled. This time they did not lunge; they pulled *together*, as a team. All four of us pulled as a team. Nobody rode on the driver's seat. Nobody yelled. Nobody cracked a whip.

The heavy wagon stirred, and the wheels made beautiful smacking sounds as they loosened from the mud. We were off! Leadership, not driving, did it!

I have never seen Lew since that day, nor have I cared to see him, but I have seen many people who used Lew's methods.

I have also had the treat of knowing some who showed the real leadership that comes, not from being in the driver's seat, but from leading. They always have full assistance on the other wheel and in the collars. They always get cooperation, not lunging.

And they are usually in the top offices, while the Lews are still in the shop.

In our world the democratic style of leading (Uncle Jack's) gets vastly better results than the authoritarian style (Lew's). The fruits of the American way of life show that the democratic style has better human relations, better production, lower costs, more loyalty.

It seems simple to be a democratic leader. All you have to do is watch these:

Ask questions	Friendliness
Be brief	Good-finding
Confident manner	Harness criticism
Directness	Increase others' self-esteem
Earnestness; sincerity	Jingle praise
	Know people

Simple as the alphabet. Yet it may require extra effort at the outset to make those practices become "second nature."

As you begin to make those practices habitual, watch your human relations rise!

LEADING AND BOSSING

Harry Selfridge was a Michigan farm boy. He started at the bottom with Marshall Field in Chicago. In ten years he was Field's partner. Later he opened his own store in London and revolutionized English store methods. As H. Gordon Selfridge, he gave his staff in London this list of contrasts between bosses and leaders.

The Boss	*The Leader*
Drives his men.	Coaches his men.
Counts on authority.	Gets their good will.
Keeps them guessing, fearful.	Arouses their enthusiasm.
Talks about "I."	Makes it "We."
Says "get here on time."	Gets there ahead of time.
Finds blame for breakdowns.	Fixes the breakdown.
Knows how it is done.	Shows how it is done.
Makes work a drudgery.	Makes work a game.
Says, "Go!"	Says, "Let's go!"

184

INDEX

185

ABOUT THE AUTHOR

Author of more than a dozen books and hundreds of magazine articles, Dr. Donald A. Laird has won wide readership as a popularizer of psychology in its application to everyday life. After receiving his Ph.D. degree from Iowa State University, he did further graduate study at Yale and then joined the faculty of Colgate. There he taught psychology for many years and also became director of the Colgate Psychological Research Laboratory. It was at this time that he began to turn out the books and articles which later were to consume all his time and interest. In the early 1940s he wrote *The Technique of Handling People, The Technique of Building Personal Leadership,* and other "technique" books which achieved large sales and brought Dr. Laird recognition as a popular writer of practical self-help books. Mrs. Laird has collaborated with him on all of his recent publications.

Dr. Laird has done consulting work for a dozen of the leading corporations in their fields, and is a Diplomate in Industrial Psychology of the American Board of Examiners in Professional Psychology.